TIME DOESN'T HEAL

Why High Achieving Widowed People Feel Stuck and
How to Rebuild a Meaningful Life

TERESA AMARAL BESHWATE, MPH

Time Doesn't Heal: Why High Achieving Widowed People Feel Stuck and How to Rebuild a Meaningful Life

Disclaimer

ISBN: 979-8-9937119-0-4

To you, dear reader. You can rebuild an incredibly good life. You can feel joy again. Doing so honors your person. You can do it all fueled by love.
Love lives.

Contents

Foreword

 "Happiness can be found even in the darkest of times if one only remembers to turn on the light." — J.K. Rowling

Teresa Amaral Beshwate turns on the light for the people who meet her and for those who read her powerful books. She has the remarkable ability to help people move forward in their lives while realizing the full magnitude of their loss.

I was widowed in 1995 when my husband and our two young sons died in a small airplane crash in Colorado. At that time, there was no network for widowed people—let alone for those who were both widowed and bereaved parents. I had to find my own way forward. I did so through trial and error, supported by family, friends, and colleagues; by reading the limited books available; by connecting with a few people who had experienced similar losses; and with the guidance of a skilled therapist. Eventually, I was able to write my own story—both to keep my family's memory alive and to gain insight into my grief journey with the hope that it might help others as well.

In 2021, I attended Camp Widow, a conference created specifically for widowed people. It was there that I met Teresa and attended one of her workshops. A whole new world opened up for me. She helped me make sense of my experiences as both a widow and a bereaved parent.

When Teresa's first book, *Life, Reconstructed*, was published, I read it in one sitting. I bought multiple copies—some to share with widowed friends and several to keep on hand to give to newly widowed people. I continue to read and reread it and each time I am reminded of a powerful truth: I don't have to believe everything I think.

So when Teresa told me she was writing a second book, it was hard to contain my excitement. I knew I would again be challenged and supported by her thought-provoking insights and that those insights would improve my life. *Time Doesn't Heal*, written for people who are two to five years widowed and beyond, spoke directly to me. The book is intentionally designed with prompts that encourage reflection and new ways of thinking. I responded to each one and learned a great deal about myself through the process.

Teresa is a highly skilled writer with remarkable insight into how to support people who have experienced profound loss. She has the rare ability to gently push readers forward while fully honoring the depth of their grief. By integrating the lessons in *Time Doesn't Heal*, I have gained a different perspective on my experiences—one that allows for more joy and less pain. This book offers hope, not by erasing loss, but by helping readers learn how to live alongside it.

Dr. Nancy Saltzman

Get the Support You Need

Keep the momentum going. Scan this QR code or go to:

https://www.thesuddenwidowcoach.com/timedoesntheal

Because your healing journey doesn't end with these pages.

Step into a space where the book comes alive—through tools, resources, and connection.

Access companion worksheets, guided exercises, seasonal support, and discussion guides designed to help you apply what you're learning.

Join others who are reading *Time Doesn't Heal*—share, learn, and grow together.

Ask questions. Find answers. Feel supported.

Introduction

In 2012, my husband, Ted, and I were out of state celebrating our wedding anniversary. We were having lunch when his heart stopped beating. Despite my best efforts, and those of first responders and the nearby emergency department, that was the day I heard the words that divided my life into the Before and After: "He died."

Ted often told me I would write a book someday. I always replied that, given all of the books ever written, I had nothing to add.

I was wrong.

In the aftermath of his death, I could find few resources that actually helped me. Which led me to write my first book, *Life Reconstructed: A Widow's Guide to Coping With Grief, Finding Happiness Again and Rebuilding Your Life*, and the accompanying journal. At the time of this writing, it has sold nearly 8,000 copies in paperback, ebook, and Audible formats, and I'm deeply honored that my words have reached so many.

With its short chapters and recurring themes, *Life Reconstructed* is ideal for the newly widowed who struggle, as I did, with reading, comprehension, and retention.

Time Doesn't Heal is ideal for those who can read longer chapters that dive deeper into the various topics of grief, no matter how long ago the loss. I've aimed to make each topic relevant for those who've been widowed for 2-5 years and beyond.

Here's how best to use this book: Read Chapter 1-6 sequentially, because they serve as the foundation for other chapters. Then, feel free to skip around.

In each chapter, take action where I've prompted, and see the accompanying journal for further application prompts. Knowing the tools conceptually is one thing, but applying them to your daily life is where the learning happens. You can read books and watch videos about snow skiing, but until you hit the slopes, it's all conceptual. The tools and concepts in this book are life changing when you apply them in your life.

I offer journal prompts throughout this book to help you apply what you're learning. You can use any notebook or journal to respond to the prompts—and I highly recommend that you do! Alternately, this book has an accompanying journal by the same name that takes these concepts even deeper. It is available on Amazon.

Contrary to popular belief, the first year does not mark the end of grief. You will not have experienced all the "firsts" after just 12 months. Grieving a spouse is to grieve your shared past, their physical absence in the present, and the loss of the future you planned. It will take years to comprehend the full magnitude of your loss.

Grief has no finish line. It's neither a sprint nor a marathon. A better analogy for grieving is hitting the gym, day after day, perfecting your technique, lifting heavier and gaining strength. At no point does someone waltz in and declare you "finished" with your strength training. The same is true with grief. It's about learning the biomechanics to shoulder it and building the strength to carry it more easily. For me, grief is like a backpack I wear all the time—but I can go weeks and even months and hardly realize it's there.

Time, in and of itself, does nothing to heal. In fact, the passing of time can actually stall healing. What heals is intentionality practiced over time. Applying what you learn in this book will help you become intentional in every aspect of your life, in grief and beyond.

Although the tools and concepts in this book can be generalized to various types of loss (and life in general), my personal experience is with the loss of my spouse, and my professional experience is helping widows and widowers navigate grief.

Scissors are a useful tool, unless we use them against ourselves. Then, they are sharp and potentially harmful objects. The same is true for every tool and concept in this book. Each can be incorrectly used against you. The correct use is to serve you, not to harm or punish you.

Rest assured that what's meant for you will stay with you. As for what isn't meant for you, simply put it right back where you found it and move along on your journey. There is no pressure to make everything fit for you.

There is no such thing as "moving on," "getting over it," or leaving your person "in the past." This book is written through the lens of integrating your person, which research shows is a helpful and healthy way to move forward. Integrating them is to include them in big and small ways, and honor them as you learn to step forward toward the differently beautiful life that's waiting for you.

No one could have prepared me, or you, for such a catastrophic loss—not to mention the fallout: the secondary losses that come, some expected, some unexpected, each packing a punch. What this book does is equip you with the tools to navigate these challenges, help you deal with anything life throws at you, and help you evolve and grow as you process your grief.

It equips you to heal.

To heal means to make your way to the place where the pain and the loss no longer control your life. To remember with more joy and less pain. To become the next version of yourself, fueled by your love for your spouse, and your spouse's love for you.

In the aftermath of something inexplicably horrible, this book urges you to leave room for the unimaginably good. To expect it, in fact, and to create it—not in *spite* of your loss, but *because* of it.

It is my deepest desire that this book lights your path to fully and intentionally living again, because you have a pulse, because the world needs you, and because your person loves you still.

Yes, your person died. But your love did not. Your relationship has changed, and also remains intact. Love lives.

ONE

Meeting This You

 "I learned a long time ago the wisest thing I can do is be on my own side."

—*Maya Angelou*

Y ou've always been the one who gets things done.

Focused.

Driven.

Capable. When life handed you a challenge, you set a goal, made a plan, and pushed through. You knew how to motivate yourself, stay on track, and deliver results—for yourself and for others who counted on you.

You made things happen. You handled it.

You are who I would call a high-achiever.

Until the day your spouse died.

That day, everything changed. Not just your life, but *you.*

In my experience, high achievers struggle the most with the loss of a spouse, and for good reasons. The tools you once relied on—checklists, grit, willpower, mental toughness—suddenly fail you.

The harder you push, the more stuck you feel. Grief is neither linear, nor categorical. There is no one "right" way through, and there is no one handing out grades.

So if you're like most high-achieving widowed people, you've started wondering: What's wrong with me? Why can't I figure this out? Am I failing...for the first time in my life?

As months go by, it can start to feel certain that you're failing. Your mind keeps collecting "proof" that you're not measuring up, while dismissing signs of progress. That's why time, by itself, can keep you stuck.

So the old adage that "time heals" is not only incorrect, the opposite is true: time can actually stall healing.

Here's the truth: You're not failing. You just need new tools for a completely different kind of challenge, which is exactly what you'll find in this book. But first things first: how you treat yourself matters.

The Most Important Relationship

Right now, there's one relationship that matters most: your relationship with yourself.

It's about how you speak to yourself, how you treat yourself.

Do you kick yourself when you're down, or do you love yourself through the hard parts?

High achieving people are often their own toughest critics, often to the point of being unkind, and sometimes downright cruel. They hold themselves to a higher standard, expecting excellence at every turn. And it gets results, as high achievers tend to be successful, efficient people.

But in grief, that mindset doesn't make you stronger; it chains you to suffering.

Spoiler alert: Love is the way forward.

Journal Prompt

Who were you before your spouse died?

List the traits and skills that defined you. Write them down.

(Please do this, even if you're "not a journaling person." This matters.)

You Are Not Your Former Self

Your spouse's death was catastrophic—so much so that it changed you, too.

The traits that served you in the past may not serve you now. That's not a personal flaw. It's the reality of losing a spouse.

You've never done this before. This part of your life requires different tools, different skills, and a different way of being—exactly what we'll build together in this book.

There are two reasons this matters. I want you to:

1. **Stop kicking yourself for not "being your old self."** It's an energy drain with no upside.
2. **Start fresh.** Consider yourself a blank slate. Get curious about the person you are now.

Grieving Is Learning

You're learning:

- Who you are now
- How you interact with friends, family, work, and the world
- How your brain currently functions
- How to navigate life without your spouse's physical presence
- How to repair, replace, troubleshoot, and decide

Write this down, because this is a key takeaway: There's no one "right" way to do this. No owner's manual. No rulebook. There is only *your* way, on *your* terms, in *your* time.

The Power of Curiosity

Curiosity is your most useful tool. It moves you forward with less judgment and more insight.

Curiosity in daily life might sound like:

- The today version of me is crying by 9 a.m. Interesting.
- The today version of me wants to skip the party and stay home. Noted.
- The today version of me feels guilty for enjoying a vacation. Okay.

Journal Prompt

What do you notice about the today version of you?

Pretend you're a scientist collecting data. No judgment, just observation.

Curiosity's Kryptonite

Curiosity is the Number 1 most important feeling to help you through grief. It has an inverse relationship with self-criticism. When self-criticism is high, curiosity is low. When you can be curious, you won't be self-critical. The default position for most high-achieving people is self-criticism. Whenever you're frustrated with yourself, kicking yourself, or otherwise giving yourself a hard time, you're in a self-critical mindset, meaning you're not able to learn. This is a spin cycle of suffering. It's important to recognize it and get yourself to a state of curiosity, which is exactly what you'll learn to do in the pages that follow.

Making New Choices

Because you're no longer your former self, you are not bound by your former self's decisions.

That might mean:

- Choosing cotton sheets instead of linen
- Ending a long-time friendship
- Finding a new hairdresser
- Overhauling your wardrobe

Everything has changed—including you.

The Today You Is Temporary

This version of you is not permanent.

One day, there will be a future you—calm, certain, living a differently beautiful life filled with meaning and purpose. Future You is calling you forward.

And because I know you want to get there as soon as possible, I invite you to make a promise

My Pledge to Myself: I am learning this version of me, who I don't know well, yet.

I am learning the truth about grief and unlearning the myths.
I am listening carefully to my own thoughts, and how I talk to myself.
I am learning to be honest and kind to myself.
I am trading self-criticism for self-compassion.
I acknowledge my efforts and thank myself for doing the hard things.
I am learning my needs, which are different now.
I give myself permission to make new choices.
I choose curiosity over judgment.
I release myself from the need to be perfect.
I am worthy of love and of the life I want.

Signature: _____

Date: _____

To summarize, time can stall healing. Curiosity is king. Self-criticism is kryptonite. You are getting acquainted with your current self, and in the chapters to come, you will learn powerful new tools for this uniquely difficult journey. You'll use them in grief, and to rebuild a differently full, differently meaningful life. One that honors and includes your spouse.

Next, it's time to deepen your understanding of your current self: brain, body and spirit.

TWO

Your Body, Brain, and Spirit on Grief

W hether your loss is recent or many years behind you, understanding how grief changes your body, brain, and spirit can help end self-criticism so you can start giving yourself what you truly need.

Grief: A Full-Body Experience

In her book *The Grieving Body: How the Stress of Loss Can Be an Opportunity for Healing*, Mary-Frances O'Connor, PhD, makes it clear that grief is far reaching, affecting the heart, immune and endocrine systems, liver and lungs, brain, and nervous system.

If you don't understand why you're not feeling better by now, *The Grieving Body* is a must-read deep dive that will help you better understand grief as a tsunami that sweeps through every corner of the body, leaving nothing untouched. (And it operates on its own timetable.)

This is why the self-care strategies that worked before your loss no longer measure up. We'll dive deeper into self-care and energy in Chapter 7.

The Injury You Can't See

If, heaven forbid, you were in a car accident, you would expect some body parts to hurt right away and others to hurt later. You would get medical tests and X-rays and necessary treatment. You would allow ample time for healing, take it as it comes, and probably rearrange your life around your physical recovery, however long that takes. You would understand that your body had been through a lot, assume that the injury is far deeper than you can see, and give your body the time and care it needed to heal.

And yet, when grief slams into the body like a tsunami, unleashing its effects on every system, it's easy to criticize ourselves for feeling utterly drained, bone-tired, and unable to summon a shred of motivation.

There is, of course, the emotional response to losing a spouse. But there is also a physiological stress response unique to grief. Increased heart rate, blood pressure, stress hormones and inflammation are all extremely common in grieving people.

Is it any wonder fatigue, brain fog, and restlessness are hallmarks of grieving?

Journal Prompt

Take a moment and write all the ways grief has impacted your physical body.

What would change if you treated your body as though it had survived a major physical injury?

Although everyone's experience is different, it can take years for the body to recover. I personally didn't experience hunger or thirst for nearly 2 years. I would size up a meal by considering how much energy it would take to chew. Digestion was difficult, sleep was evasive, and exhaustion was a way of life.

Adding to that, I found myself in a spin cycle of self-judgement. Shouldn't it be better by now? I must be doing this wrong.

Which is to say that I was throwing salt into the wound.

By "the wound" I mean the pain of loss and grief's impact on the body, brain and sprit. It's that which comes with the territory of losing a spouse.

By "the salt," I mean self-criticism—the kicking myself because I wasn't better yet, wasn't handling this well, and was unable to recognize myself. Sound familiar?

The first step to healing a wound is to stop throwing salt in it. And the way to do that is to fully understand the impact grief has on the body (and brain and spirit) and figure out how to tend to the body's current needs with unprecedented self-care (more on this in Chapter 7).

Journal Prompt

In what ways might you be adding salt to the wound?

How might you more intentionally tend to your physical body?

When Your Brain Can't Keep Up

 "My mind is like someone emptied the junk drawer onto the trampoline."

—Author Unknown

My friend Amy Florian is a thanatologist. Thanatology is the scientific study of death and the losses brought about as a result. Amy often gives a presentation to newly widowed people called, "You're Not Crazy. You're Grieving." In it, she normalizes the many behaviors that convince grieving people that they've fully lost their minds. As she moves point by point through her presentation, there's a collective sigh of relief among her audience. I never get tired of watching it.

If you're frustrated with yourself, if you think you're crazy or otherwise losing it, here's what you need to know: Your person died and everything changed, including and especially your brain. It functions differently now. You don't yet know all the ways. You're learning your own brain, no matter how long ago your person died. There's a learning curve, which means the most useful feeling is *curiosity*.

What will *not* help you is to kick yourself, dish out some "tough love," or otherwise put additional pressure on your grieving brain.

Mental Toughness Doesn't Work

Arguably, getting tough with yourself has its place. Grief is not where that works. In fact, being tough on yourself while you're grieving will keep you stuck and suffering. It will make your brain perform even worse. It adds unnecessary stress, which impacts not only your brain, but your body.

What will help you is to better understand how your brain is working these days. It will work better in the future, rest assured. But what

25

you've got right now is the brain you've got right now. The task at hand is to better understand your current brain, observe it objectively, and find practical ways to better support it.

Journal Prompt

What changes have you noticed in your thinking, memory, or focus since your loss?

To help you get and stay in curious observation of your own brain, in this chapter, I'll highlight a few main ways the brain functions differently in grief and how to best support it. Chapter 21 dives deeper into common and normal brain tendencies.

Your Brain Is Baffled

First, your brain understands the world with your person physically in it. It is genuinely confused by their absence, and it must rewire itself to understand this new reality. To quote Dr. O'Connor in *The Grieving Brain,* "The idea that a person simply does not exist anymore does not follow the rules the brain has learned over a lifetime."

You know that your person died. And simultaneously, your brain doesn't fully understand that they died. You look for them in a crowd, or listen for the garage door to open, or pick up your phone to call or text them. This is your brain operating on what it's known to be true for the years you've spent with your person: that they are physically present.

Here's an unrealistic but simple example. You go to college for 10 years, taking a full load each semester, and getting a B in every class. Your grade point average is a solid 3.0. Then you get a single A (or an F). Your

GPA doesn't budge because there are too many data points that make it a solid 3.0.

Your brain is a bit like this GPA, not reflecting your new and unwanted reality because too many data points suggest otherwise.

What your brain needs is to collect more data points to eventually catch up, to realize and comprehend what has happened. This doesn't happen overnight. It isn't time itself that helps, but specific experiences over time.

For example, having coffee alone is foreign at first. After having coffee alone day after day for many months, the brain starts to catch on. New experiences stack up new data points.

Journal Prompt

Describe one everyday activity that feels foreign without your person—and how it's slowly becoming more familiar.

On the other hand, let's say you travel just one time a year. If your person has been gone only 3 years, then you've probably only traveled twice, which means you've come home to an empty house only twice. Your brain hasn't had much experience in this area. Which is why your brain might anticipate your person picking you up at the airport, or might expect to see them at home when you arrive. You know your person passed 3 years ago, but you haven't had much experience coming home after a trip. It's not the passing of time, but the *experiences* we have as time passes, that brings our brains up to the present reality.

Your Primitive and Higher Brain

Let's look more specifically at two parts of the brain and how they operate in grief: the primitive brain—focused on survival—and the prefrontal cortex— focused on planning, reasoning and impulse control.

Primitive Brain: The Overzealous Neurologic Bodyguard

The primitive part of the brain has just one job, which is to keep us alive. It does this in three simple ways, known as the "Motivational Triad":

1. Avoid pain
2. Seek pleasure
3. Be efficient

The Motivational Triad is hard wired into us. No one is exempt, not even high achievers.

Another important characteristic of the primitive brain is that it is Version 1.0. It hasn't evolved since the early days when danger was truly around every corner. It's designed to keep us safe in the cave. No matter that the cave is cold and dark—at least it's familiar. Familiarity, to the primitive brain, means safety.

Imagine a muscle-bound, anxious, overzealous bodyguard doing his best to keep you in the cave. He's cute, he means well, and sometimes his services are needed.

Anytime you've been in actual danger, it was your primitive brain that took over and got you back to safely. If you think back to such a time, notice that you didn't overthink it. Your primitive brain acted quickly and instinctively.

This is because when the primitive brain is running the show, the prefrontal cortex falls silent, which is by design. If you found yourself on a busy street with oncoming traffic, it wouldn't make sense to pause, think about various options, consider what you'd like to have for lunch, and make a mental note that you're meeting a friend at the gym later.

No, the primitive brain recognizes danger, takes complete control, and gets you back to safety.

The loss of your person sent your primitive brain into overdrive. The person most important to you died. The worst-case scenario happened. There's almost nothing more threatening to your primitive brain. Even in the "best" of circumstances, your primitive brain is on overload, dominating your thinking, searching for any possible sign of danger, activating your nervous system, and therefore shutting down your prefrontal cortex. It's as if your already overzealous bodyguard is now over-caffeinated.

That means that you're overhearing your own panicky primitive brain chattering away, on repeat, every waking hour. Your thoughts likely focus on fear, scarcity, how you "did it wrong," and why this can't possibly be your reality.

You may notice yourself stuck in thought loops—repeating the same story, asking the same questions, coming to no conclusions—on rinse and repeat.

Your brain may spend time in what's called "counterfactual thinking." This kind of thinking sounds like, "If only X, then Y," where X is some action you could have taken, and Y is that the outcome is different: Your person is still alive. This is your brain trying to rewrite the story, and in doing so, feeling some control over the outcome. It's a mini-escape of sorts from your unwanted reality.

Journal Prompt

Write down every fear, worry, or "if only" thought running through your mind today—no editing. Just get them out.

You may notice moments of the prefrontal cortex trying to join the conversation, but it's like a spotty dial-up internet connection at best. Add to that, it can create conflict. It might sounds like, "There must be more to this life than this mediocre, mundane existence." "I don't want to stay stuck here forever." "I don't want to spend the rest of my life alone." It's a gentle whisper that says, "there is more."

Enter the conflict: "But how can that be when my person died? Doesn't that mean leaving him behind, moving on, forgetting him? That sounds disrespectful."

And in rushes your muscle-bound, well-intentioned bodyguard, ushering you back into the cave. What's familiar is miserable, he explains, but at least it's safe.

Prefrontal Cortex: The Adult in the Room

Your prefrontal cortex is essentially the part of your brain that allows you to "adult." That is, when it's operating at full capacity. Grief knocks the prefrontal cortex offline, but bringing it back online is possible. Rebooting the adult, thinking part of your brain requires:

1. Noticing the primitive brain chatter
2. Thanking your primitive brain for doing its job
3. Calming the nervous system.

Perhaps you've never needed to know how to calm your nervous system before, or maybe strategies that once worked for you are not currently helpful. It's a matter of experimenting and learning what's best for your current self.

The ideas below are not one-size-fits-all, but they're worth experimenting with so you can find what works best for you.

Breathing techniques. There are countless breathing techniques and the internet is full of helpful information. It's worth trying a variety of techniques to find what work best for you. One easy one to start with is to take a big inhale and then stretch your exhale out for twice as long; if you breathe in for four counts, breathe out for eight. It's worth experimenting to find techniques that you like and find calming.

Meditation. There are wonderful resources for meditation and mindfulness for those who are grieving. The apps Insight Timer, Calm, and Headspace are just a few resources, and all of them have free trials you can use immediately. There are also many free guided meditations available on YouTube.

Prayer. If you're a praying person, pray when you are overcome by fear or panic. It was incredibly helpful for me. You do not have to practice a particular faith, or even consider yourself particularly religious, to benefit from a prayer practice.

Grounding techniques. These are techniques that engage the 5 senses to help you manage fear and return to the present moment. They also help you regain a sense of control and reduce the intensity of emotions. Even focusing on one sense can help. Try breathing through your nose; notice the cool air rushing in with each inhale and the warm air blowing out with each exhale.

Bilateral stimulation. Like many breathing techniques, bilateral stimulation is a simple approach that will likely go unnoticed by others. Simply pass any small object from one hand to the other, across the midline of your body, until you feel calmer.

Physical activity of any kind can help. In *The Grieving Brain*, Dr. O'Connor writes of her own personal experience with panic, "The only thing that helped me during panic was matching my physical activity to the amount of adrenaline my body pumped out...." My client Hanna found relief in twice-daily hot yoga sessions. For other people it's lifting weights, or taking long walks. For me, it was learning Krav Maga.

There is no one "right" way to calm your nervous system. There is simply the way that works for you at this time. Know that your grief will change with time, and your nervous system–calming strategies might need modification.

Journal Prompt

List three calming practices you've tried since your loss.

Which worked best?

Which ones might you try next?

Depending on the nature of your loss, consider the help of a therapist trained in EMDR or brainspotting to help you deal with trauma. EMDR stands for "Eye Movement Desensitization and Reprocessing," and it's a trauma-specific therapy based on the same concepts as the bilateral stimulation I mentioned above; there are a variety of ways to deliver EMDR, not just eye movement. Brainspotting is another trauma-specific treatment that does rely on eye positioning. These trauma-specific tools were exactly what I didn't know I needed to help calm my nervous system and process my grief. I wish I had found them sooner. It would have very likely prevented a great deal of suffering over several years.

As your nervous system becomes calm, your prefrontal cortex can come online and stay online for longer periods of time. If you're a praying person and on speaking terms with the Divine, invite a collaboration with your prefrontal cortex. You can also just speak directly with that part of your brain.

The Compassionate Leader

Your prefrontal cortex is an advocate for your future self. It thinks about the future, and it knows what's best for you. It's like a calm and compassionate leader walking her team through difficult times, toward a bright future. This is the voice you hear when you're talking to yourself (rather than listening to yourself), when you're thinking true, useful, kind thoughts, on purpose. More on this in Chapter 6.

Supporting the brain you currently have is a trial-and-error experiment of various strategies.

Getting Real with Expectations

Your expectations matter. I remember thinking, "This must be what it's like to have had a stroke. I know my brain isn't working, and I can't make it work."

It's actually a decent analogy. Grieving brains are detectable on functional MRI, and approaching my brain as if I had had a stroke was helpful to me. It meant that I didn't know how my brain would work. I needed to learn it anew. I needed to do things differently as it recovered, to expect less of my brain. I needed to do anything I could to support it. I knew it would get better eventually, and I realized that being mad that my brain wasn't working would significantly slow its progress.

If Former You accomplished 10 tasks per day, expect Today You to accomplish just two. If today your brain is capable of accomplishing more, great. By expecting only two tasks to get accomplished, you've removed the pressure of 10 tasks, and prevented the self-criticism and meaning-making that would follow when you couldn't get it all done. Meaning-making could sound like, "I must be getting dementia," "I'm never going to get better," "I'm going to be fired from my job," or any number of other panicky brain chatter from your overzealous bodyguard.

Journal Prompt

What is one expectation you can lower for your brain this week?

With projects that required multiple steps, I learned to leave myself notes detailing what I had accomplished, what the immediate next step was, and the steps that followed that. It saved me from having to reorient myself and start from scratch the next time I picked up the project.

I bought a carabiner and attached it to my keys. This way, my keys were either hanging on the hook by my door, or hanging on my purse if I was away.

It helped my brain to declutter my environment, get rid of junk mail immediately, to put paperwork in the filing cabinet as soon as possible, and to leave only papers that needed my attention on my desk.

Journal Prompt

What thoughts is your brain offering you? The primitive brain is a bit like a toddler trying to get your attention. Give it your undivided attention, and let it tell you everything it's deemed important. Write it all down. Journaling those thoughts will calm your chattering brain once it is heard, and will give you a record of your whereabouts that you will look back on to appreciate your progress.

Put Post-It notes where you need them, or set reminders and alarms on your phone. To this day, I put appointments on my digital calendar that remind me of what I need to bring with me when I leave the house.

My loss changed my ability to tolerate a noisy environment. In the early years, I simply avoided loud places. Today, I notice that if I'm not well rested, it's harder to tolerate noise. I have a few sets of custom ear plugs that provide the buffer I need. One came from the local hearing aid store, and the others from a vendor at a trap-shooting event. One pair is equipped with Bluetooth technology so I can listen to calming music or white noise as needed.

Some of the strategies I learned in the early years of grief are still excellent ways to support my brain today, 13 years later, and I'm more efficient because of these practices.

You'll find some adaptations will be short term, and others long term. I don't judge myself; I simply find ways to support my brain's needs. That's my hope for you: Observe your brain, withhold any judgement, and experiment with ways to support the brain you have today, knowing that, in the future, it will work better.

Journal Prompt

What ways can you better support your brain?

Your brain will recover on its own timeline, not yours. It's like living in the central valley of California, where the winter fog descends and ascends on its own schedule. At first, the fog is thick and seems to be permanent. But you will find that it does lift, and gradually it will stay lifted for longer intervals. Notice that. And when it descends again, don't make extra meaning out of it. Instead, tell yourself, "This is the part when the fog descends, and that's the way of it." Being mad about the fog doesn't make it ascend any sooner. It will lift in its own time. Be gentle with yourself and your brain.

When the Spiritual Ground Shifts

 "What makes each loss so catastrophic is its devastating, cumulative, and irreversible natural."

—*Jerry Sittser*

When Faith Feels Fragile

In my experience, the loss of a spouse shakes the foundation of our spiritual self. The most devout may suddenly find themselves questioning the God they once trusted without hesitation. Lifelong nonbelievers may feel drawn to mysteries they once rejected. And many find themselves somewhere in between, navigating a spiritual landscape they no longer recognize. Almost every widowed person I've met can point to a moment, or a season, when their spiritual life shifted—sometimes in a whisper, sometimes in an earthquake.

Journal Prompt

Has your loss caused you to question, reconsider, or deepen your beliefs? Write about one moment, thought, or conversation that made you aware of this change.

Which spiritual practices or beliefs still feel meaningful to you? Which ones no longer fit—and why?

Questions Without Answers

It's okay to step back and question everything. It's okay to feel betrayed, unable to trust in the divine goodness you were once certain of.

It's okay to be furious, to feel cheated out of the life you signed up for.

It's okay to be angry that prayers for healing had no effect. (And it's okay to feel envious that for someone else, prayer worked.)

It's okay to question why bad things happen to good people.

It's okay to demand answers, "Why him? Why us? Why not some serial killer?"

I remember sitting at my step-daughter's high-school football game near a dad with a pulse who was complaining about having to be there, and thinking, "*Really*, God?" Followed by instantaneous regret for thinking such a thought.

Journal Prompt

Write down every spiritual or existential question you're holding. Don't try to answer them. Just notice what's there.

There's No Right or Wrong

Many people are conditioned to heavily monitor and quickly judge thoughts and feelings related to spirituality as "right" or "wrong." That judgment can create a spiral of shame and self-criticism, limiting the ability to learn and grow.

I personally had many temper tantrums, throwing myself on the floor, spiritually speaking, and having complete meltdowns. I was angry. I felt I could no longer trust the God I had relied on since childhood. Eventually, I decided we were no longer on speaking terms.

All the while, I knew that if a parent could love a tantrum throwing toddler and patiently wait for that toddler to pick themselves up off the floor, then God was surely doing the same for me.

I want to offer that it's okay to think whatever you think, and it's okay to feel anything you feel. In the next chapter, I'll explain default, unintentional thoughts, and in Chapter 6, we'll explore chosen, intentional thoughts. This will help normalize and neutralize anything you're thinking and feeling unintentionally, and create space to think and, therefore, feel, on purpose.

Journal Prompt

If there were no "right" or "wrong" way to grieve spiritually, what would your next step be in tending to your soul?

If you could speak honestly to God (or to the Universe, or whatever feels right to you) without fear of judgment, what would you say?

In his classic book, *A Grace Disguised: How the Soul Grows Through Loss,* Jerry Sittser, who lost his wife, mother, and young daughter in a car accident, writes, "It is therefore not true that we become less through loss—unless we allow the loss to make us less, grinding our soul down until nothing is left but an external self entirely under the control of circumstances. Loss can also make us more. In the darkness we can still find the light."

I believe that grief does grind away at the soul, and that's the way of it. In my experience, finding the light starts with noticing and normalizing the reactions your spiritual self is having to the loss of your spouse. Remember from Chapter 1, grieving is learning, and we can't learn when we're spiraling in self-criticism.

Thoughts, On Purpose

Then, it's about choosing true thoughts on purpose. More on this in the chapters that follow.

Today, my chosen thoughts are that my husband was only on loan to me. He was mine to love in this life. He was mine to walk home. And yet I never truly lost him. He is mine to love now, always, forever and after. Likewise, he is loving me still, present tense, because love never dies. Our souls are connected and will always be.

I still don't know why he died. I won't have that answer in this life. But I do know that love lives, and that is where I focus my thoughts.

Journal Prompt

What true, comforting thought could you choose on purpose today about your person or your relationship? Write it down as if you fully believed it, and notice how it feels in your body.

THREE

The Model

 "Nothing ever goes away until it teaches us what we need to know."

—Pema Chodron

T he loss of a spouse feels like being dropped into some surreal existence, as if you're living someone else's life. It's chaotic and deeply painful, and almost nothing seems to make sense.

Enter a tool called The Model. It was developed by my coach instructor Brooke Castillo to capture the key basis of Cognitive-Behavioral Therapy. CBT is an approach that uses thoughts to change feelings and behaviors, and The Model is my favorite tool to make it accessible to everyone.

Whether you're brand new to life after loss or years into the journey, The Model can help you. It's a simple yet powerful tool that works for every human—grieving or not—and it will change the way you see yourself and your life. Used correctly, it will help you view every aspect of your life objectively, and without criticism. Let's begin.

Journal Prompt

Think about one moment in the past week that felt especially chaotic, surreal or challenging. Write it down in as much detail as possible, without trying to make sense of it yet. Just capture what happened.

Why to Use The Model

The Model brings order to the chaos of loss. It's a logical and practical way to categorize all things, and therefore to see the cause and effect of everything that is happening. When we can better understand what is, we can become the architect of what we want (more on that in Chapter 6).

The Model brings clarity to life after loss and life in general. It's a universal tool and one you'll want to use forever, in grief and beyond.

The Model has five parts: circumstance, thought, feeling, actions, and result.

How to Use The Model

Using The Model is simply a matter of categorizing things based on the following definitions.

Circumstances are the factual things that happen. They can be proven in a court of law, and all people on Earth would agree that they are true. Examples include that your spouse passed. Sister-in-law said words. Friend sent text message. Relative has not called. Circumstances are pure fact. They're best stated briefly, neutrally, and to the point. To keep The

Model simple, specific and clear, there is only one circumstance in each Model.

Journal Prompt

Pick one thing that happened recently. Write it down as a pure fact—no opinion, no emotion, just what could be proven in court.

Thoughts are sentences in our minds. When a circumstance happens, the brain offers thoughts. It's what brains do. There are no "good" or "bad" thoughts. I don't think it's useful to categorize thoughts as "positive" or "negative." What is incredibly useful is to categorize thoughts as default (unintentional) or intentional.

Unintentional thoughts are a lot like an unattended jukebox that plays songs on default. It's what jukeboxes are designed to do. And, you can tell a jukebox what to play. The analogy ends here, because unlike a jukebox that has a finite number of songs to choose from, we humans have an infinite number of thoughts available to us.

Unintentional thoughts happen, and they always will. You are not your thoughts; you are simply the observer of them.

Researchers say that we humans think about 60,000 thoughts each day. Eighty percent of those thoughts are negative (which is a *human* statistic, not a *grieving* human statistic.) And ninety percent of those 60,000 thoughts are repetitive, playing like a broken record.

So, an overwhelming majority of unintentional thoughts are negative and well practiced. But here's what they are not:

- They are not necessarily true.
- They are not necessarily useful.
- They are not necessarily kind.

In the words of my wise client Minnie, "The first pancake usually goes to the dog."

Intentional thoughts, on the other hand, are both optional and infinite. We humans have the ability to think true, useful, kind thoughts, on purpose.

And if there are an infinite number of thoughts available (there are!), then why not think intentional thoughts that are true, useful, and kind? More on intentional thoughts in Chapter 6.

Each individual Model has only one thought. It must be a short sentence or a phrase. If the thought is a sentence with a comma, it's too long and should be broken up into two separate sentences and therefore two separate Models.

Journal Prompt

For that one circumstance you wrote down, list every thought that came to mind in the moment. Don't edit—just capture them all. Select just one thought *to put into The Model.*

Feelings are sensations in the body, caused by the thought you're thinking in that moment, whether consciously or subconsciously. I dive deeper into feelings in Chapter 4. For now, notice when you feel frustrated, for example, and ask yourself, "Why do I feel frustrated?" The answer will be the thought on your mind in that moment. My brain's habitual source of frustration is the thought, "There's shouldn't be so much traffic."

Connecting thoughts and feelings is a powerful and helpful skill, in grief and in life. Once you get into the habit of making this connection, you'll never want to forget it. It's transformational.

For simplicity and clarity, each Model has only a single one-word feeling.

Journal Prompt

Name one feeling (one word only) that comes up when you think the thought you just wrote down in your Model. Where do you feel that sensation in your body?

To review, circumstances are factual things that happen, and they prompt thoughts, which are sentences in your brain. Then, thoughts cause feelings that you experience in your body.

Feelings, in turn, drive action (or inaction). Any action you've ever taken was due to how you were feeling in the moment. If you went to the gym, you were likely feeling motivated or deliberate. If you stayed in bed, perhaps you felt overwhelmed or sad. If you sent a scathing text message, you likely were feeling angry.

Although each Model has only one thought and one feeling, a Model should have as many actions as come from the feeling in the previous line of the Model. The more the better. (See example next page.)

Journal Prompt

From that one feeling, what actions (or inactions) do you tend to take? List as many as you can, even small ones.

Actions (or inactions) aggregate to create results, which is the fifth and final component of The Model. For example, you step on the scale and the number you see is the result of several actions: what you've eaten, how much you've exercised, whether or not you've gone to the grocery store, etc.

Another example of a result is a college degree, which required a multitude of actions to achieve. Let's look at this scenario in The Model.

- **Circumstance:** Career path (factual)
- **Thought:** I want to help people by becoming a nurse (short sentence)
- **Feeling:** Deliberate (one-word feeling)
- **Actions:** Take prerequisite courses, apply for nursing school, register for classes, buy books, study, decline social invitations, take exams, study for boards, pass boards (several actions that happen from the feeling of "deliberate")
- **Result:** Become a registered nurse (result of various actions above)

The thought always appears in the result line in some way. In this case, the thought "I want to help people by becoming a nurse," resulted in becoming a nurse.

The Model has a few rules that keep it simple and powerful:

- **Circumstance:** Facts only, keep it neutral.
- **Thought:** Brief sentence or phrase.
- **Feeling:** One-word feeling.
- **Actions:** All of the actions and/or inactions that come directly from the feeling above.
- **Result:** The product of the various actions above, that reflect the thought.

Journal Prompt

What result do all those actions add up to?

How does it connect back to the thought you started with?

Keep It Simple

Of course, we humans have tens of thousands of thoughts, and a variety of feelings in any given day. If you're experiencing three different feelings, then that is three different Models. If you have two thoughts running on repeat in your mind, that is two different Models.

The Model is a fundamental tool for decoding and categorizing what's happening in your life—both externally and internally. It reveals how you respond to the events around you, making your reactions easier to see and understand.

Don't Use The Model Against Yourself

Remember that in Chapter 1, you pledged you would avoid self-criticism. That promise is important as you put the Model into use. To quote Steve Jobs, "If you define the problem correctly, you almost always have the solution." The Model teaches that you are not the problem. "The problem" is simply a chain of events caused by a circumstance, which prompted unintentional thoughts, which created a feeling, which drove actions that piled up to create a result. There is actually not a problem at all, but there is a result that you can clearly see, and then decide if it's right for you, or not.

Like every tool and concept in this book, The Model is to be used *for* you, not against you. It's designed to help you bring order to your life, see the cause and effect at play, and discover the control that you do have in your own life. It is not to be used for self-criticism, which will prevent you from learning and will just keep you stuck and suffering.

Journal Prompt

Think about a recent situation where you were hard on yourself. If you used The Model for it without any self-criticism, what would change?

When to Use The Model

The Model will help you when:

- You can't put your finger on what's bothering you.
- You don't understand yourself.
- Life feels messy, confusing, and chaotic.
- Someone said something hurtful.
- Your dearest friends haven't called to check on you.
- Your supervisor at work is demanding.
- You feel stuck.

- You feel incredibly lonely.
- You had a great time and now you feel guilty.
- You lack a sense of meaning and purpose.
- You can't seem to break a habit.
- You can't seem to create new habits.
- You want to want to, but when it comes down to it, you don't want to.
- Deep down, you want to find someone special to share your life with, but it seems incorrect, impossible, or incredibly challenging.

The Model brings incredible awareness to the past as well as your current situation, thoughts, feelings, actions, and results. This is the first step, and this type of Model is called the Unintentional Model. It helps you to better understand where you were and where you are, so that you can make your way to where you want to be. (More on that in Chapter 6.)

The Model is a wise teacher, a gentle messenger, and the most ideal curriculum for you in this exact moment. The same Unintentional Model will keep showing up in your life until you've gained every ounce of wisdom from it, until you're ready for the next Unintentional Model to appear. It's a never-ending leveling-up of self-awareness and growth.

 "Life is a mirror of your consistent thoughts."

—Napoleon Hill

Journal Prompt

What is one piece of wisdom you've already gained from noticing your unintentional thoughts, feelings, actions, and results?

FOUR

Feelings

 "Feelings are like children. You don't want them driving the car, but you shouldn't stuff them in the trunk, either."

—Author Unknown

The Trouble with Trying to Stuff Emotions

Many people were taught as children to stuff their uncomfortable feelings in the trunk. They heard constant messages such as, "Don't be nervous," "Don't be sad," "Chin up!" In essence, they were taught that difficult feelings aren't okay.

It's not uncommon for a new client to say, "Feelings? I'm supposed to know how I feel?" Most people have practiced stuffing feelings away for decades. What does it even *mean* to feel?

This chapter will help you to identify feelings, their source, and their impact.

Journal Prompt

What messages did you receive about emotions when you were growing up?

Which of those still influence how you handle feelings today?

Feelings: An Inside Job

A feeling, otherwise known as an emotion, is a sensation in the body. Feelings are caused by thoughts. In turn, feelings prompt actions, which create results.

Notice that feelings come from thoughts—your thoughts. They don't come from another person's words or actions, from your performance review, or from the glaring absence of your best friend who promised to be there for you. Circumstances like those happen, and then you have a thought about them, and that thought in your own brain is what causes a feeling.

Journal Prompt

Think of a recent moment you felt upset. What thought was on your mind right before that feeling?

This means that all feelings are always an inside job. Which is the best news, because feelings are 100% within your control. Not the unintentional ones—those happen by default—but the intentional ones. (More on this in Chapter 6.)

Useful Ways to Label Feelings

Humans experience a wide range of feelings and it's tempting to judge and label them in some way. I don't find it useful to label them as "good" or "bad," "positive" or "negative." But here's what *is* useful: Feelings can be described as comfortable and uncomfortable. There are useful and not-useful feelings. There are feelings that happen due to unintentional, unexamined thoughts, and there are feelings that happen due to intentional, examined thoughts.

Journal Prompt

List three comfortable feelings and three uncomfortable feelings you've experienced this week.

Which were useful?

Which weren't?

Feelings vs. Fight or Flight

While a feeling is caused by a thought, whether conscious or subconscious, a nervous system response is an automatic, physical reaction. Fight, flight, freeze, and fawn are the body's responses to fear, stress, and trauma. These are instinctive, survival responses when your primitive brain perceives danger.

To fight is to face the threat with assertive or aggressive behavior. **Flight** is to flee, which can look like physical or emotionally withdrawing. **Freeze** is to become paralyzed or unable to act. And **fawn** is to appease the threat by becoming overly agreeable or submissive, or sacrificing one's own needs.

When your nervous system is triggered, you don't feel safe—no matter whether you are in real, physical danger or just imagined, hypothetical danger. Calming your nervous system is top priority before attempting to process a feeling, which I cover in the next sections. Refer to the "Calming the Nervous System" section in Chapter 2 (page 31).

Why to Process a Feeling

> *"It is an act of bravery to feel your feelings."*
>
> *—Gayle Forman*

Once I spoke to a tearful woman whose husband had passed 25 years prior. At the time of his passing, she had a career she loved. She retired and enjoyed meaningful pursuits and later moved to an assisted living community full of enjoyable things to do. But in 2020, she found herself bound to her room due to the COVID-19 pandemic, and the feelings came crashing in. Twenty-five years' worth of difficult feelings hit her like a ton of bricks.

Sooner or later, feelings demand to be felt.

The truth is, in all those 25 years, she never escaped the feelings. She never truly avoided them. All that time, she was experiencing something much worse than the pain of loss. She was experiencing the pain of loss *plus* her fear of the pain, *plus* self-criticism, *plus* regret, *plus* anger, plus, plus, plus…

She expended monumental amounts of energy to stay on the run, to resist the inevitable. All the while, the predator chasing after her grew to massive proportions, which naturally made her all the more fearful.

I said, "You must be exhausted." She replied wearily, "You have no idea."

What she experienced for 25 years was exponentially worse than the pain itself. I understand, because I did it, too.

I don't want that for you.

Journal Prompt

Is there a feeling you've been avoiding? How have you been keeping it at bay, and at what cost?

Before I tell you how to process a difficult feeling, I want to further make the case for why you should. Why it's life-altering. Why it matters, now more than ever.

Here are my top 10 reasons why processing a difficult feeling is incredibly beneficial:

1. Override the brain's fear of difficult feelings. (More on this in Chapter 5.)
2. Utilize and strengthen the prefrontal cortex.
3. Honor the feeling.
4. Bear witness to the feeling.
5. Tend to the feeling.
6. Learn from the feeling (because feelings are messengers).
7. Gain mastery over the feeling, allowing difficult feelings to exist.

8. Reduce the feeling to proper proportions.
9. Increase your confidence in your ability to feel a difficult feeling.
10. Help you to use feelings to your advantage.

If I had only known how to process a difficult feeling (and why it's so important), my journey would have been significantly easier. I hope I've convinced you why it's so beneficial to process your own difficult feelings.

Journal Prompt

From the list of 10 reasons to process a feeling, which one matters most to you right now? Why?

How to Process a Feeling

Set a timer for anywhere between 90 seconds and 2 minutes.

1. Notice how difficult the feeling is. Rate it on a scale of 1 to 10, where 10 is the most uncomfortable feeling you've ever felt.
2. Remind yourself that this feeling is coming from a thought. Therefore, you're not in actual danger.
3. Breathe. Take deep breaths of the feeling to invite it in.
4. Name it if you can: What are you feeling now? If you're not sure, simply move on to Number 5.
5. Notice its location. Where is this feeling in your body?
6. Notice its properties. Does the feeling have a particular shape?
7. If the feeling were a color, what color would it be?
8. Is this feeling hard or soft?

9. Is this feeling in motion? If so, is it fast or slow?
10. How does this feeling make you want to react?
11. Why are you feeling this? What is the feeling trying to tell you? If the answer doesn't come easily, don't get stuck here. Proceed to step 12.
12. Rate the feeling again on the scale of 1 to 10.

Repeat steps 1-12 and notice how the feeling changes over time.

Journal Prompt

Choose one feeling you're experiencing today and walk yourself through the 12 steps in this section. What changed by the end?

Faster processing. If you're not in a position to do the 12 steps above, there are faster ways to process a feeling. For example:

1. Place your hand on your heart and take two deep breaths, each with a long exhale.
2. Bilateral stimulation: Pass any object from one hand to the other until the feelings lessens.
3. Fast tapping: Use two fingers to tap the top of your head, then between your eyebrows, the side of your eye, beneath the eye, and your breastbone; then grab your wrist with your palm facing you, take a breath, and exhale twice as long as you inhaled.
4. Other ways to process a feeling include writing/journaling, music, movement, crying, art/creative outlets, massage, or coaching. Notice other methods that work for you.

Journal Prompt

Which "fast" processing methods have you tried? Which felt most effective?

Feelings Are Habitual

When we think of habits, we often think of actions that we habitually take. But feelings can be habitual too. When you wake up filled with anxiety, before you've had a chance to think your first thought, anxiety is likely a habitual feeling.

You probably know people who are in a constant state of overwhelm, or people who are always stressed. And you might know people who always seem to be calm, cool, and collected, or always upbeat.

Ninety percent of the thoughts we think are redundant and repetitive. Given that thoughts cause feelings, it makes sense that feelings are repetitive too—habitual.

Human brains are hard wired for efficiency, so they're always seeking the path of least resistance. In life after loss, this means that the brain will offer you thoughts that lead to overwhelm—because when we're over-whelmed, we don't tackle that pile of paperwork, we don't return the phone calls, we don't cook a meal. Overwhelm leads to doing nothing, and doing nothing is consistent with the brain's desire for efficiency, because doing nothing is an efficient way to conserve energy.

The same is true for worry, anxiety, and confusion. These feelings don't lead to any productive action. The brain will habitually offer thoughts that create these feelings, again in an effort to conserve energy. It's not your fault; it's primitive hardwiring.

But thanks to our prefrontal cortex, we can override this primal default setting and instead create useful feelings that drive productive action. More on this in Chapter 6.

Journal Prompt

What feeling(s) seem to be your brain's "go-to" lately? What actions are happening because of these feelings?

The 50/50 of Life

I want to offer you the notion that life is 50% uncomfortable emotions and 50% comfortable emotions. Does this ring true for you in your life before loss?

When I first heard this concept, I didn't think it was true for me because I was extremely happy in my life before loss. But when I factored in how I felt in traffic, when I was running late, troubleshooting technology, dealing with a difficult co-worker, or after I had been transferred three times while waiting for customer service only to be disconnected, I started to wonder if the 50/50 might be accurate.

Life after loss feels more like 100% uncomfortable emotions, at least in the beginning. Eventually you'll experience both uncomfortable and comfortable feelings.

Duality

The truth is that comfortable feelings coexist with uncomfortable feelings. It's called duality, and while I'm sure it exists in life before the loss of a spouse, in my experience, it's far more obvious after.

Sometimes we experience two seemingly conflicting, but equally true, feelings in the same moment. "Bittersweet" is a good example.

Sometimes we experience them sequentially—a moment of happiness is followed by a moment of shame.

Journal Prompt

Looking at the past month, what's an example of a comfortable and an uncomfortable feeling you experienced in the same day, or in the same moment?

Honoring with Joy

It's easy to think that the only way to honor your person is to feel uncomfortable feelings. For years I thought that if I wasn't miserable, then I didn't love him enough.

But if the shoe were on the other foot, I certainly would not want my husband to think that feeling miserable was the one and only way to honor me.

Today I know that I honor him with my joy, with my happiness, and with my laughter. I honor him as I build a life that I love, as I grow, as I realize my capacity, as I reach my goals.

Journal Prompt

If your person could choose how you feel most of the time, what do you think they'd want for you?

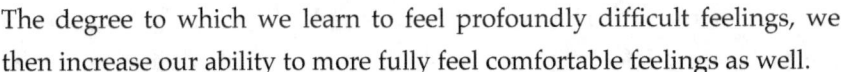

The degree to which we learn to feel profoundly difficult feelings, we then increase our ability to more fully feel comfortable feelings as well.

Maybe Kahlil Gibran said it best in his classic *The Prophet*, when he wrote, "The deeper that sorrow carves into your being, the more joy you can contain."

Or put another way, by an author unknown to me, "Life is so ironic. It takes sadness to know what happiness is, noise to appreciate silence, and absence to value presence."

Both comfortable and uncomfortable feelings can be useful. This morning I didn't feel like lifting weights. But I felt determined—the kind of determined that comes from self-discipline. Which didn't exactly feel good, but it got my workout done.

A few years ago, I read scripture and a eulogy for a family friend's funeral. I quite naturally felt sad that day, and I wanted to feel sad. I wanted my words to come across with an appropriate level of emotion. Sadness isn't a comfortable emotion, but it was natural, appropriate, and useful for me that day. It spared me from wasting loads of energy trying to hide my sadness.

Journal Prompt

What's one uncomfortable feeling you're willing to practice allowing this week, knowing it can't harm you?

If we understand that life is a mixture of comfortable and uncomfortable feelings, then we don't resist the uncomfortable. We don't make ourselves wrong for feeling it. We can simply acknowledge that this is the part when I feel uncomfortable feelings, and that's the authentic human experience. It makes discomfort less uncomfortable.

To quote my coach instructor, Brooke Castillo, "When we feel harder, we suffer less."

We can make ourselves wrong for feeling discomfort, or we can simply feel it as it comes.

Stepping outside of what is familiar is never going to feel comfortable. Instead, it might feel uncertain, uneasy, nervous, or anxious. In this case, these feelings are both uncomfortable and useful.

To the degree that you learn to process uncomfortable feelings, you'll be able to allow yourself to feel uncomfortable feelings without it being scary, and without it stopping you from taking the next step toward the future that is waiting for you.

FIVE

The Human Response to Difficult Feelings

A s we discussed in the previous chapter, attempting to dodge pain is a whole other level of exhaustion. It's futile, and it makes the load exponentially heavier.

This is true of any type of pain or discomfort, whether you're grieving or not. It's normal and natural to try to dodge discomfort. In this chapter, you'll learn about this hardwiring in greater detail, which will allow you to understand yourself better. The goal is to trade self-criticism for curiosity so you can take efficient strides forward.

The Three Dodge Tactics

It's our primal instinct to avoid pain. That's a survival instinct and it drives us to try any number of ways to dodge it. In fact, there are three main ways we try to dodge painful emotions: resisting, reacting, and avoiding.

First, we resist difficult feelings. That means we try to sweep them under the rug, or refuse to acknowledge them. It's a bit like trying to hold a beach ball under water- you can do it for a while, but it is exhausting and at some point, the ball emerges. We don't do this deliberately; it's instinctual.

Journal Prompt

What is one feeling you tend to resist?

How do you know you're resisting it?

Another way we attempt to dodge difficult feelings is by reacting. This looks like emotional outbursts or impulsive behavior, like rash decisions or self-destructive actions. We aren't aware that we're trying to dodge the pain, because the reaction happens so fast.

Journal Prompt

Think of a recent time you reacted quickly to something. What feeling might you have been trying to avoid?

The third way we try to dodge difficult feelings is to avoid them entirely. This is attempting to numb or "buffer" the pain with things like overeating, overdrinking, overspending, overscrolling, overscheduling, overcommitting, binge watching, and other excessive behaviors.

It's any type of activity that (a) attempts to avoid or numb the pain and (b) has its own negative consequence. For example, weight gain, hangovers, financial problems, exhaustion, etc. Once again, these actions are automatic, driven by our primal instincts to avoid pain. We are hard-wired this way because pain could mean danger.

Journal Prompt

Which numbing or avoidance habits do you recognize in yourself?

What short-term comfort do they give you, and what long-term cost do they have?

The Extra Weight We Carry

Most of us have the pain of our loss, plus the pain of our attempts to dodge it, which is its own heavy load. We lump them together, because we can't easily distinguish between the two. So it just feels like this massive weight to carry. It's like carrying rocks in your purse.

And the more we run from the pain, the bigger it gets, the more we fear it, and the faster we try to run. It's just as the German proverb says: "Fear makes the wolf bigger than he is."

I spent 6 years on the run. My avoidance strategy of choice was staying overly busy. My job required a lot of travel, I came home to 10 acres of work on my ranch, and then got back on the next outbound plane.

From Avoidance to Facing the Pain

I thought the pain was so great, that if I felt it, I wouldn't be able to recover. I remember the moment I realized I had nothing left, no ability to outrun it. That was when I saw I had no choice but to face what I'd been avoiding.

If you're riding a horse and a dog chases you, the rule of thumb is that you turn to face the dog, and even move toward the dog. When the dog is giving chase, it's big and bold. When faced with a thousand-plus-pound horse moving in its direction, most dogs quickly shrink back to original proportions and apologetically turn tail and head for home.

The same is true with difficult feelings. When we actually face them—the mere act of *deciding* to face the pain— we set down any resistance, any attempt to avoid what we need to feel. By facing it, we no longer react to it. The pain no longer dictates our actions, because we're willing to look at it and process it.

Journal Prompt

What is one painful feeling you've been afraid to face?

Imagine turning toward it instead of away. How might that change its size?

And so what we actually face is the pain itself, without any extra layers of heaviness. It's pain in its pure form.

And compared to the effort it takes to dodge it, compared to how *frightening* it is when we're *trying* to dodge it, the pain in its pure form is remarkably less burdensome. It's still heavy, but it's not one ounce heavier than necessary.

Our Expanding Capacity to Feel

Our souls have the capacity to expand as a response to pain. In *A Grace Disguised*, Jerry Sittser, quoted earlier, writes, "Loss can enlarge its capacity for anger, depression, despair, and anguish, all of which are natural and legitimate emotions whenever we experience loss. Once enlarged, the soul is also capable of experiencing greater joy, strength, peace, and love."

Facing the pain that comes with loss is to bear witness to it, to tend to it, to process it. And when we do that, the pain loosens its grip. It lightens, dissipates, maybe even leaves entirely.

In Chapter 4, I shared how to process a difficult feeling. You can also listen to this process in Episode 4 of my podcast, *Life Reconstructed: A Widowed Way Forward*, available on all major podcast platforms and through my website (thesuddenwidowcoach.com). This skill is a super-power, not only for grief, but for life.

Journal Prompt

What would be possible for you if you felt less fear of uncomfortable emotions?

SIX

The Intentional Model

 "May your choices reflect your hopes, not your fears."

—Nelson Mandela

C hapter 3 introduced the concept of The Model, and specifically the Unintentional Model, which is a tool to map out the cause and effect of a specific situation either in the past or the present moment.

This chapter takes The Model to the future tense and reveals a very practical way to create anything your heart desires. This is useful in grief and in life in general.

Do you want to have more confidence, clarity or courage?

Would you like to feel more productive, energized or focused?

Are there actions you'd like to be taking, or habits you'd like to break?

The Intentional Model is the answer.

Think of one area of your life where you'd like more confidence, clarity, or peace. Write it down as your starting point for this chapter.

The Three-Step Foundation

First, create an Unintentional Model using the guidelines in Chapter 3.

Create as many Unintentional Models as you need to help you better understand your current situation. Remember, only one thought and one feeling per Model.

Process the feelings you're experiencing in those Models. This is an important step that is tempting to skip (because brains are hardwired to try to dodge pain), but here's why it's incredibly important: Feelings are messengers. Processing feelings in your Unintentional Model will help better inform your Intentional Models.

Journal Prompt

Review an Unintentional Model you've created recently. Have you truly processed the feeling in it, or have you been tempted to skip that step?

When we don't process a difficult feeling, we prevent ourselves from accessing high-quality intentional thoughts. It's a bit like shopping in a thrift store; there are some very nice items, but it requires a lot of sorting through the lower-quality merchandise to find the good stuff.

In contrast, by processing unintentional feelings first, we can then shop at the equivalent of Neiman Marcus for higher-quality intentional thoughts.

Journal Prompt

What difficult feeling might you need to process before you can think differently about your situation?

So to recap:

1. Create an Unintentional Model.
2. Process the feeling you're experiencing in that Model.
3. Refuse to be self-critical.

Remember the pledge you signed in Chapter 1? It matters here.

American psychologist Carl Rogers said, "The curious paradox is that when I accept myself just as I am, then I can change."

Self-criticism prevents curiosity. And curiosity leads to learning and growth.

No Judgment—Just Cause and Effect

As you look over your Unintentional Model, just normalize it. Normalizing sounds like this: "This circumstance happened and then my brain offered me this default thought, which naturally led to this feeling, which drove these actions, which led to this result." It's a normal downstream flow: cause and effect, no judgement.

Remember, brains offer thoughts. An overwhelming majority are negative and repetitive. We don't get to pick the default thoughts (at least not directly). We do get to pick intentional thoughts, and that's exactly what we're doing in this chapter.

Designing the Future with The Intentional Model

The *Unintentional Model* helps you to understand your past and present self better.

The *Intentional Model* helps you to grow, challenge yourself, and create literally anything you want. You can put any result you truly want for yourself in the Result line, and then complete the rest of The Model to help you achieve it.

Now, am I at 5'4" going to ever play in the WNBA? Absolutely not. In my heart of hearts, do I want to play in the WNBA? Also no.

What I truly want is to serve more widowed people through my work. That's what resides in my ever-evolving Intentional Model.

Journal Prompt

What is one specific result you'd like to create in the next 6 months? Write it in the Result line of a blank Intentional Model.

One of many benefits of the Intentional Model is that it helps you see the control you have, even in life after loss. We often cannot control circumstances, and we can't control our unintentional thought, but we *can* control the intentional thought we choose to think, on purpose.

The same rules apply as in Chapter 3: The circumstance must be factual, provable in a court of law, and all people on Earth would agree that it is true. When creating an Intentional Model, the circumstance should be the same as in the Unintentional Model.

The thought is a short sentence or phrase. The feeling is a one-word feeling that comes from the thought. The actions are as many actions or inactions that naturally come from the feeling. The result is the product of the various actions, and a reflection of the thought.

In the case of the Intentional Model, the thought is chosen, on purpose. It's hand selected and tried on for size.

The Gatekeepers of Intentional Thinking

Intentional thoughts should have three gatekeepers:

1. Is it true?
2. Is it useful?
3. Is it kind?

Thoughts are infinite. We have an infinite number of intentional thoughts to choose from. So why not choose thoughts that are true to you, useful for your life, and kind to your body, mind, and spirit?

If you're a praying person, choose intentional thoughts prayerfully. Invite Divine collaboration and allow intentional thoughts to bubble up from your soul.

Or simply put your brain to task. Ask it to brainstorm, and do your best to keep it on task. Ask it for 25 possibilities.

Journal Prompt

Think of one new thought you'd like to practice. Does it pass all three tests?

The intentional thought is, after all, the first instance of complete control we have. And since thoughts cause feelings, which drive actions, which create results, then four-fifths of the Intentional Model is completely within your control.

It All Starts with a Thought

Albert Einstein is quoted as saying, "We cannot solve our problems with the same thinking we used when we created them."

Mental flexibility is your ability to analyze, question, and adapt your thinking. It is the most powerful tool in life, and especially in life after the loss of a spouse. Brains offer 60,000 thoughts a day. Eighty percent of those 60,000 thoughts are negative, and 90% are repetitive. The first step is to monitor your own thoughts (expect them to be glass-half-empty and redundant). Then, mental flexibility means challenging your default thoughts, and choosing true, useful, kind thoughts, on purpose, to replace them.

Aristotle said, "It is the mark of an educated mind to be able to entertain a thought without accepting it." I would suggest that it's also the mark of a flexible mind.

Your brain will always offer you a default thought. As you raise your awareness, you become a better eavesdropper on your own thinking so you're more aware of default thoughts.

Next, you're learning to challenge the default thought. My client Gladys, who is now a coach herself, is a master at noticing her default thoughts and immediately considering whether the opposite might be true. She's a good example for all of us.

Ask yourself:

- What if the complete opposite is true?
- How could the opposite be true?
- What else might be true?

The default thought is a lot like your high school debate team. Let's call it Debate Team A.

To challenge a default thought, ask yourself, "What does Debate Team B say?"

Your default thoughts mainly come from the primitive part of your brain, which is hardwired to keep you alive by urging you to avoid pain, seek pleasure, and conserve energy. This is the nature of default thinking.

These are the thoughts that you overhear. That panicky primitive brain offers fear and scarcity—which isn't a problem. In fact, that means your brain is functioning according to its design.

Intentional thoughts, on the other hand, are chosen thoughts. Choosing thoughts is more like talking to yourself rather than listening to yourself.

A good guideline is to talk to yourself more than you listen to yourself.

Journal Prompt

Write down a current default thought.

Then write three alternative thoughts—including the complete opposite—and see how each feels.

Notice when your brain offers you scarcity: "There's not enough time." "There's too much to do." "I don't know how."

Mental flexibility is to counter these thoughts with abundant thinking. "There's plenty of time for what matters most." "I'll just do the next logical thing." "I can learn how."

Journal Prompt

List three scarcity thoughts you've had recently.

Write an abundant counterpart for each one.

The Intentional Model teaches that choosing a true, useful, kind thought is the most important part; then, the rest of the Model flows downstream naturally—because thoughts cause feelings, which drive actions, which create results.

Your Belief Plan

It is a tremendous help to create a list of intentional thoughts that are true for you, serve you well, and are kind. I call this a Belief Plan.

Belief Plans should be used proactively and reactively. Start your day brushing your teeth and reading your Belief Plan, pausing after each intentional thought to feel the feeling that comes. Over time, these thoughts will come naturally and habitually. But for now, they need proactive practice.

Journal Prompt

What's one intentional thought you could tell yourself every morning that would shape your day for the better?

When your brain offers default thoughts that are possibly untrue, not useful, and unkind, grab your Belief Plan and review it. This is a good reaction when old thoughts arise.

Balance your "airtime," between default (unintentional) thinking and intentional thinking. Said differently, spend plenty of time listening to Debate Team B.

To use another analogy, rather than listening to an unattended jukebox play songs that you don't like, tell it what to play. Give it your most favorite playlist and let that be the soundtrack of your life after loss.

Journal Prompt

If your mind had a "favorite playlist" of intentional thoughts, what five thoughts would you want on repeat?

Below I offer an intentional thought brainstorm. This is quite literally food for thought, and not all suggestions directly relate to grief. I want to help you get started, with the ultimate goal of training your brain to brainstorm intentional thoughts that are true for you, serve you well, and are kind to you.

As you read the list below, try each thought on "for size," and see how it makes you feel. Does it ring true for you? If some aren't a fit, simply leave them right where you found them and continue along your unique path.

How do you know if a thought serves you well? See how it plays out in The Model. How does it make you feel? What actions would naturally flow from that feeling? What result would those actions create? Would you like that result? You get to decide.

Intentional thought brainstorm:

- I am guided.
- I am exactly as I should be.
- Everything happens right on time.
- God/the universe doesn't make mistakes.
- I am not my mind. (I am the *observer* of my mind.)
- Love is always an option.
- Unconditional love is something I do for myself.
- I'm responsible for everything I think and feel.
- No one can cause an emotion inside of me.
- People are allowed to behave the way they want; I am allowed to react the way I want.
- It's not what I do; it's who I am.
- There's nothing I can do that wouldn't be worthy of forgiveness.
- There's nothing wrong with me.
- I am enough.
- Nothing has gone wrong here.
- We're here to get to the work of ourselves.
- My purpose is the life I'm living now.
- I am deeply loved.

- The world longs for what I have to offer.
- There's nothing I truly want that I can't have.
- Hard work feels amazing.
- I can do hard things.
- Familiarity is not the same as comfort.
- Suffering is sometimes familiar, but not necessary.
- Worry serves no purpose.
- Money is easy.
- There's plenty of time.
- I could do twice as much. Everything I do is a choice.
- My past is perfect.
- There's nothing they can do to make me happy; that's my job.
- What I do doesn't make me happy; what I think does.
- I don't have fun; I am fun.
- What I look for I will find.
- What others think of me is about them, not me (good and bad).
- Trying to get someone to love me in order to feel love is like trying to get someone to eat for me to feel full.
- Everything is as it should be.
- It was meant to happen the way it did.

 "Finally, brothers and sisters, whatever is true, whatever is noble, whatever is right, whatever is pure, whatever is lovely, whatever is admirable—if anything is excellent or praiseworthy—think about such things." —Philippians 4:8

SEVEN

Protecting Your Energy with Self-Care

G rief changes everything, including the way we use and conserve energy. What once came easily now feels heavy, and even the simplest tasks can feel monumental. Life after loss requires more energy than before, and grief itself drains so much of it. That's why self-care isn't optional; it's essential.

Self-care protects your energy, makes room for healing, and ensures you have something left to give—to yourself and to those you love. And because you are not the same person you were before loss, the way you care for yourself must also change.

Learning Yourself Anew

Think of this chapter as an invitation to get reacquainted with yourself. The strategies that may have supported you before loss may no longer work for who you are now. Former You had different needs; Current You is starting from scratch. What restores you now may surprise you. What drains you may catch you off guard. To discover this, you'll need a curious, beginner's mindset—one that assumes you don't yet know what self-care looks like in this season, but that you are committed to finding out.

It's tempting to assume you already know how to care for yourself, but I encourage you to make no assumptions. First, because self-care likely wasn't your top priority before loss. And second, because the kind of care you need today is not the kind of care you needed then. You are learning yourself anew—your current brain, body, spirit, and energy levels.

Along the way, remember the pledge you made in Chapter 1 to be kind to yourself, set down self-criticism, and stay open to discovering who you are now. These promises matter deeply as you get acquainted with your current self, which will require that you notice what drains you, experiment with what restores you, and slowly build practices that fit the life you're living now.

Self-Care Isn't Selfish

Because self-care can seem selfish, let's distinguish between the two.

To be selfish is to be overly concerned with your own needs, regardless of others, and sometimes at the expense of others.

Self-care, on the other hand, is tending to your own needs. In doing so, you become a better version of yourself, which causes a ripple effect, positively impacting others.

Selfishness is at the expense of others.

Self-care positively affects others.

Self-care isn't selfish.

Journal Prompt

What beliefs do you hold about self-care being "selfish"?

Where did those beliefs come from?

When you take care of yourself, how does it positively affect the people you love?

Saying Yes to Yourself

Sometimes self-care requires saying, "No," to others, but by saying, "No," to others, you say, "Yes," to yourself and your needs. Practiced over time, self-care has a positive effect on the people you love.

So saying, "No," in the short term allows for the best version of you to emerge over time, benefitting those you love. Saying, "No," often prompts an uncomfortable feeling, which can be processed using the prompts in Chapter 4. The more you process difficult feelings, the more you can allow them to be with you, in their proper place: in the back seat of the car *you're* driving.

Finding and Plugging the Energy Drains

I notice that whenever I update my phone, the battery drains faster. I can plug it in, of course, but I always wonder what's draining the battery in the first place.

This is true with cell phones and in life—and specifically in life after loss. To best care for ourselves and manage microscopic energy levels, we need to find and plug the energy drains. I'll touch on the eight most common drains I see in widowed people. For the topics that resonate the most, feel free to skip ahead to the chapters I reference below.

Drain 1: People Pleasing. Even as you exist in the devastation of having lost a spouse, it's common to find yourself attempting to please others. There are good reasons for it. It's a well-intentioned attempt to control someone else's thoughts and feelings. But by prioritizing the needs of others over your own, it adds suffering on top of the pain. Chapter 8 offers a closer look at relationships and people pleasing.

Drain 2: Dodging Feelings. Attempting to dodge difficult feelings is both instinctual and energy draining. You know you're doing this when you find yourself on the run—binging your favorite show, staying overly busy, overeating, overdrinking, overscrolling, and the like. To spare your energy, notice your primal urge to dodge difficult feelings, refuse any self-criticism, and then choose to process feelings instead. More on this in Chapter 5.

Drain 3: Socializing. Social situations can be a massive energy drain, even for the most outgoing of extroverts. You go, even though you don't want to. Small talk gets awkward fast. You don't feel like you fit in anymore, and conversations that were once interesting now seem irrelevant. In Chapter 8, I offer tools to navigate such situations.

Drain 4: Expecting People to Behave Differently. Life would be much easier if only this person would do this, or say that, or in the name of all that is holy, *stop* doing this and *stop* saying that. Expecting people to behave differently is a large-scale leak in your energy levels. In Chapter 8, I reveal why we do this and what to do instead. It's life-changing.

Drain 5: Carrying Anger and Resentment. Anger and resentment are heavy emotions, and although they're quite natural, they are also optional, no matter the circumstances. In Chapter 9, I explain further and, when you're ready, I'll show you how to set them down.

Drain 6: Arguing with Reality. We all argue with reality, and we get to do it for as long as we want. It sounds like, "This should have never happened to him...to us." "We should be living the retirement years that we planned for and looked forward to." "I should have been able to save her." Arguing with reality is normal, and also extra painful and exhausting. We'll take a close look at arguing with reality in Chapter 11, which will help you plug this energy drain when you feel ready.

Drain 7: Decision Fatigue. The process by which you once made decisions is likely no more. Now, a host of decisions need to be made, from the first moments of loss and thereafter. Fear of making the "wrong" decision is real, and paralyzing. There is hesitation for good reason, and yet decision fatigue is a slow leak of energy. In Chapter 12, I offer a fresh perspective on decisions, along with a process you can use to prevent decision fatigue.

Drain 8: Guilt and Regret. Guilt and regret are heavy, energy draining, and also optional, no matter the circumstances. We often confuse these two feelings, but they are unique. In Chapter 10, I'll help you find the root cause and show you the way to plug this drain in an authentic and effective way.

Journal Prompt

Which of the eight drains do you notice most in your own life right now?

How could you begin to gently plug that drain this week?

Recharging Your Batteries: Brain, Body, and Spirit

Plugging the energy drains goes a long way to preserving energy. Next, let's take a fresh look at how to charge your batteries and how to proactively keep them charged.

It's useful to think of ourselves as having three "battery packs:" brain, body and spirit. Sometimes my brain is in the red, but my body has some energy left. Sometimes it's my spirit that needs recharging. There is certainly overlap among the three, but thinking of myself as having these individual battery packs has helped me to learn what needs recharging and how to go about it.

I'll share my recharging techniques to give you food for thought. It's my hope that you will experiment with a beginner's mindset as you learn the techniques that recharge you, brain, body, and spirit.

My **spiritual batteries** are recharged in a number of ways. Silence, solitude, and nature are key. My Catholic faith is a major source of spiritual recharge. A certain amount of time on the back of my horse and spent with my dogs do wonders for my spirit, along with being with the people I love.

When I find my **brain batteries** in need of recharge, I know I need to move my body. I aim to get more sleep. I take note of how hydrated I am. I may need to dial in my nutrition. Meditation, journaling, and getting coached all quiet the mental chatter. It also helps me to read a book that offers a unique perspective, new information, or just entertainment.

When my **body batteries** are in the red, my go-to sources of recharge are prioritizing sleep, taking a day off from lifting heavy weights and opting for stretching as my workout, or postponing any hard physical labor on the ranch and choosing easier tasks instead. Nutrition and water intake matter here, too.

Sleep is a challenge for many grieving the loss of a spouse. There are a number of quality resources available on this topic. It's a matter of finding what helps you. I struggled for the first several years after my loss. I noticed that when I hadn't slept, my brain offered an array of doom and gloom the following day. I learned to put my brain on notice:

"If I haven't slept well, I hereby will not believe anything I think today. All decisions will be postponed until after a good night's sleep."

Journal Prompt

What seems to restore your spirit these days?

What activities will you experiment with to recharge your brain?

What practices boost your physical body's battery pack?

Proactive Energy Management

Proactively charging my batteries boils down to my calendar. Former Me, if invited to three social events on a Saturday, would have found a way to attend all three. Current Me may say no to all. I've learned that on errand day, I max out at three stops. I try to schedule when traffic is light.

It helps me to look at my weekly calendar and notice whether I'm tending to my battery packs. My calendar needs downtime so that I can find myself brushing Cooper, my Great Pyrenees, or grooming my horse's mane or pruning rosebushes—all of which I find recharging.

I schedule time to create content that will help widowed people, and to learn how to grow my business so I can reach more people.

I schedule time to walk my almond orchard, time to lift weights, and time to just be.

If I plan to be in a crowded, noisy environment, I balance that out with big doses of silence and solitude the next day.

Former Me had completely different needs. Well, honestly, I probably didn't really know what she needed. I've learned what my current self needs, what her limits are, what will drain her, and, therefore, what needs to be scheduled to recharge. But it's always evolving, I am always getting a little smarter as to my needs, and sometimes I slip back into old habits and need to course correct.

So, how about you?

Journal Prompt

How could you adjust your calendar or daily rhythm to better protect your energy?

What boundaries might you need to set (with yourself or others) to keep your batteries charged?

You may choose to think of your battery packs differently than I've suggested. There is no right or wrong. What matters is that you have a curious mindset and use trial and error experimentation to learn yourself:

1. What drains you
2. How best to recharge your batteries
3. How best to keep them proactively charged.

And then, give yourself permission to keep evolving your approaches, because *you* are evolving. Your grief is ever-changing. As you learn, you will fine tune your strategies.

Taking good care of yourself has never been more important. Right now, your assignment is you. Tend to you.

Journal Prompt

What's one new self-care experiment you'll try this week?

How will you know if it's working for you?

EIGHT

Relationships and Finding Your People

 "If you really want to get along with somebody, let them be themselves"

—*Willie Nelson*

Think about the person who frustrates you the most. Wouldn't it be nice if they would just change? Life would be simpler, easier and more peaceful if they would correct their behavior, right?

Any time we are frustrated by another person, they are failing to meet our expectations of them.

The Manual: Hidden Rulebooks

We have expectations for all the people in our lives. In fact, we have a secret rulebook for how we expect a person to behave. It's called The Manual.

Manuals sound like:

- "They need to realize that I'm not 'over it.'"
- "I can't believe it. She told me that it's time to 'move on.'"
- "He should have never asked me out so soon after my husband's passing."
- "They shouldn't have offered to help me if they weren't going to actually help."
- "They should have invited me to the party."
- "She should be supporting me."
- "They should realize that I'm still grieving."
- "They should know what I need."

Most often we don't actually tell people what's in our Manual for them; we just expect that they should know.

And if only they would follow our Manual for them, then we would get to feel...differently. Perhaps seen, validated, understood, supported, loved.

Journal Prompt

What are some "should" statements you catch yourself thinking about others?

Who in your life are you currently hoping will act differently?

The Pain of Expectations

While it seems like having expectations of other people is normal, it is actually the source of great pain because it makes our feelings dependent on the actions of another person. It robs us of our power. It gives other people power over us. It prompts us to try to control others so that we can feel better.

Journal Prompt

How has expecting someone to behave differently caused you extra suffering?

What feeling would you get to feel if only that person would change their behavior?

Letting People Be Who They Are

Fortunately or unfortunately, adults have the freedom to behave however they choose. My Number 1 tip for the people who frustrate you is to let them behave exactly as they behave. Expect them to behave exactly as you know they behave. Make a mental bingo card, with each square denoting how you know this person to behave. When they behave accordingly, mentally mark the square. This puts you in an observational mode, in sync with reality, which means you're much less likely to react.

People who haven't lost a spouse don't understand the journey. Those who show up try to say the "right" things and sometimes they say the most unhelpful things. They don't know what your needs are. Some don't reach out in the spirit of giving you space, or for fear of saying the wrong thing.

In fairness, we were once in their shoes, and we also didn't know what we didn't know.

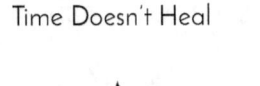

Journal Prompt

What might change for you if you expected people to act exactly as they have always acted?

How does it feel to consider letting others be wrong about you?

How We Feel Is an Inside Job

And here's another truth, for better or for worse: It's our own thoughts that create our feelings. How you feel is an inside job, dependent only on your own thoughts—not on the behavior of another.

Notice your thoughts, and know that your thoughts create your feelings. Here's a pro tip: The feelings you would get to feel if only other people followed your Manuals are the feelings you need to create more of for yourself.

If we throw away our Manuals for other people, they can no longer disappoint us with their behavior. We can let people act exactly how they act. We can stop expecting them to understand what they can't possibly understand. We can stop holding them accountable for how we feel.

That's not to say that we shouldn't set boundaries when necessary, and I'll cover that in the next section.

Other People's Manuals for You

But while we're on the topic of Manuals, it's also important to note that every person in your life has a Manual for you: how you should act, how you should grieve, what you should and should not say... That you should be further along in your journey or that you've launched impulsively and foolishly into your next chapter. You should cry more or cry less. You should have it together by now or you have it too together, therefore you must not have loved him enough.

Given that everyone has a different Manual for you, it would be impossible to follow them all. You probably don't even try to. But probably there are Manuals you do try your best to follow.

Journal Prompt

What are some examples of other people's Manuals for you in your grief?

Which ones are you most tempted to follow, and why?

The Trap of People Pleasing

Attempting to follow other people's Manuals is a form of people pleasing, which is an attempt to control them with the very best of intentions. If you follow their Manual, you believe that you are helping them to feel better, to worry about you less, to rest assured that you are okay. It's common to think that our actions can directly control other people's feelings.

But it's just not true.

No matter our actions, other people get to think whatever they choose to think—which creates their feelings, which prompt their actions.

We can lose weight and one person will think we're too thin, while another will think we are looking healthier. We can go out on a date and for every person who thinks that it's a good idea, there will be another who thinks it's too soon. We can break down in tears and one person will think we should be "over it" by now and another will think that we should cry more often.

Journal Prompt

When have you tried to manage someone else's feelings by changing your behavior?

Did it work? How did it affect your energy and peace of mind?

Living for You

You can live your life trying to follow other people's lengthy and conflicting Manuals, or you can live your life for yourself.

You can decide what's good for you and then have your own back.

You can recognize that you have absolutely no control over other people's thoughts or feelings.

You can decide that you're not responsible for how much or little other people worry about you.

You can stop seeking approval and acceptance from outside of yourself.

Because feelings come from thoughts, how you feel is an inside job. That means that how other people feel is their own inside job.

As kids, most people learned from parents and teachers to seek approval from others. But now, we're adults. We may have received acceptance and approval from our husbands, but now, we're widowed. We have perhaps spent our lives "outsourcing" our feelings, but now, it's time to bring it in-house. It has always been an inside job, after all.

Journal Prompt

If you stopped trying to control others' thoughts or feelings, what freedom might you gain?

What does it mean to "have your own back" right now?

Boundaries

My guess is that nearly everything you've read about boundaries is actually a covert attempt to control other people. This is not that.

Boundaries are only needed when someone is violating your physical or emotional space. This looks different for everyone. You get to decide what feels like a violation of your physical and emotional spaces. Here are some examples.

A violation of physical space might be when someone walks into your home without knocking. I was once in the grocery store and someone walked up to me quickly and got very close to me and asked for money. This was, for me, a violation of my physical space.

A violation of emotional space, for me, is when a someone treats me or another person rudely or disrespectfully.

What is unique and important about the definition of a boundary is that other people get to behave exactly as they choose to behave. And, if that behavior violates your physical and/or emotional space, then it's time to set a boundary.

Here's an example. If you prefer that your visitors call ahead before dropping by, a boundary would sound like this, "If you come to my home without calling first, I won't answer the door."

Notice it is not, "Don't come to my house unannounced." That would be attempting to control someone's behavior.

Instead, it is, "Do whatever you want. You can come to my house if you want to. But if I'm not expecting you, I simply won't answer the door."

Let's say you don't allow smoking in your car, because you consider it a violation of your physical space (or whatever other reason, because, after all, it's your car). A boundary would sound like this: "If you light a cigarette in my car, I will pull over and ask you to get out, because there is no smoking in my car." Again, it's not, "Don't smoke in my car." You're not trying to control anyone's behavior. You're giving them free will to behave as they please.

When a boundary is needed, it sounds like this: "Behave as you want, but if you do X (violation of physical or emotional space), then I will do Y (consequence)."

And you must follow through with the Y. Yes, it feels uncomfortable, but you're learning that discomfort is part of the human experience. Plus, this discomfort pales in comparison to the pain of losing your spouse. You can do this.

Navigating Social Situations

 "I am under no obligation to make sense to you."

—*The Mad Hatter*

Why Social Situations Feel So Hard

Social situations are challenging for many widowed people. As you learn how to navigate life after loss, you're also relearning how to interact with people, and how much energy it takes to do so. No one could have prepared you for this. Be gentle with yourself as you learn. This section will help.

The more you learn about grief, and the more you get to know your current self, the better you'll be able to navigate friendships and social situations. The more you love your decisions, the less you'll need others to love them. Learning about yourself and learning how to love your decisions is exactly what you're doing as you apply the lessons in this book.

This learning curve is a process. You won't learn it all overnight. This section offers practical tools that will help you right away.

Journal Prompt

What feels most draining to you about social interactions right now?

How do you usually feel before, during, and after being around people?

Checking Your Energy Before You Go

First, before you attend a social event, check your battery levels (see Chapter 7). Do you need to recharge your batteries instead? You may need to decline, even if you RSVP'd that you would attend.

Or, you may want to attend for a few minutes and see how it goes. (Be sure to park accordingly.)

It takes courage to walk in alone. Perhaps someone will meet you and walk in with you. It may help to remember that you likely attended some gatherings by yourself before your loss. Take a deep breath and remind yourself that this is not the hardest thing you've ever done.

Journal Prompt

What signals tell you your "batteries" are too low for socializing?

How might you give yourself permission to leave early—or not attend at all—without guilt?

When Conversations Turn Awkward

Soon, you find yourself in conversation. It doesn't take long to realize that, in life after the loss of a spouse, conversations can get awkward fast. Conversations with non-grief-savvy people, that is.

You know those well-intended people who want to fix you so they can stop worrying about you. The people who think tough love might be an effective approach. The ones who tell you that you have do any number of things, like stop wearing your wedding ring, start dating, or leave your person in the past and "move on already." Or just come to this party, or start volunteering, or get a dog.

Or the ones who ask intrusive questions, offer age-old platitudes, or compare your loss to theirs.

And the ones who ask the question that widowed people hate the most, which is, "How are you?"

These conversations are tough to navigate, so I want to offer some tips to help you. Because while sometimes you can avoid someone in the grocery store, other times you find yourself face to face with a person who just doesn't get it and you may need to interact with them.

Journal Prompt

What types of comments or advice frustrate you most?

How do you usually respond—and how would you like to respond?

A Conversation Stopper

Here is a sentence that comes in handy in a lot of the situations. I think of it as a conversation stopper, and it can be delivered with kindness: "I don't expect you to understand what this is like for me. In fact, I'm glad you don't."

It's a polite way of letting the person know that, in this moment, they're demonstrating a lack of understanding because they simply don't get it. Which is understandable because there was a time when you didn't get it, either. The only way to get it, is to experience it. And you don't want that for them.

Even if the person has had their own loss, they don't know *your* loss. Every person is unique, every marriage is unique, and every loss is unique.

This sentence works in a lot of situations, especially when someone is trying to fix you, tell you what you should be doing, and offering platitudes that aren't helpful. You can respond with, "I don't expect you to understand what this is like for me."

It's ironic that, in the most difficult chapter of life, we have to let people be wrong about us. We have so little energy to spare; if we spend what little we do have trying to explain ourselves to people who simply don't get it and can't get it, then the energy is gone. Letting them misunderstand you is sometimes the best option. It's not easy to do, but it may be the best way to save your limited energy for more important tasks.

Journal Prompt

How does it feel to imagine saying, "I don't expect you to understand what this is like for me"?

In what situations could you use this sentence to save your energy?

Handling Intrusive Questions

Now, let's look at intrusive questions. This is something my late husband taught me: When someone asks a question that feels intrusive, respond with, "Why do you ask?" This does two important things. It buys you time to think about how you want to handle it. And second, it makes them take ownership of their own question.

Then, you may choose to respond with, "I'm not ready to talk about that," or "I'm not up for discussing that with you."

Another option is to offer no response whatsoever. My uncle was recently asked an intrusive question and he simply stared at the person and allowed for a long, awkward silence until she changed the subject. Silence may be the best solution.

Journal Prompt

What's one question you've been asked that felt intrusive?

If you could redo that moment, how might you respond differently?

Answering the Dreaded, "How Are You?"

Now, perhaps the most awkward of all is also the most simple and common question, "How are you?" Sometimes the person genuinely wants to know the answer. Sometimes they don't.

You may wonder if you should be honest, or keep it to a simple response. And if you're honest, where does the conversation go from there? And how do you even answer that question when, since your loss, you've been on the roller coaster of emotions? Here are some simple responses that may help you:

- "I'm doing my best and that looks different every day."
- "I'm doing the best I can in the most difficult situation I've ever faced."

It may help to reply with a timestamp, such as:

- "Well, today is okay so far."
- "Today has been rough for me."

- "It's not been an easy morning."
- "In this moment, I feel sad."

Journal Prompt

Which short responses feel most natural for you right now?

How honest do you want to be in different settings (with acquaintances vs. close friends)?

Saying No and Keeping the Door Open

Finally, what do you say when you're invited to a party and you don't have any energy or desire to go? You can say, "Thank you for thinking of me. I won't be able to make it, but please ask me again. I would appreciate being invited in the future."

If you're not sure if you'll be able to go, you can say, "Every day is different and I can't predict how that day will go. I'll do my best to attend, but I can't make any promises."

Journal Prompt

What words feel comfortable for you when you want to decline an invitation?

How can you remind yourself that saying, "No," today doesn't mean, "No," forever?

Investing Energy Where it Matters

I hope these practical tips will help you interact with not-so-grief-savvy people. And, I strongly encourage you to expand your friend circle. I know, it's the most difficult chapter of your life and you don't have an abundance of energy. But in this book, you're learning how to plug energy drains and recharge your batteries, so that you can have enough energy for what's important. Finding grief-savvy people is an excellent use of energy.

Journal Prompt

Who in your life feels grief-savvy and safe?

Finding Your People

 "Sit with warriors. The conversation is different."

—*Author Unknown*

The Loneliness After Loss

After the loss of a spouse, even those who love you don't understand you. They can't accurately see you. They don't know how to sit with you, to be with you as you grieve.

With good intentions, they try to coax you toward what they think should be the next phase of your healing.

They offer platitudes. They try to fix what can't be fixed.

We're all a product of a non–grief-savvy society. It's foreign and uncomfortable, and we just don't want to talk about it. We can't possibly be a good support for something we don't understand.

And besides, it's impossible to truly get it—unless you've experienced it. I once didn't get it either. None of us got it, until, unfortunately, we did.

Journal Prompt

Who did you expect would support you after your loss? What actually happened?

How have unmet expectations added to your grief?

The Secondary Loss of Relationships

One of the many things that you least expect when you lose your spouse is that the people who you thought would be there for you, the people who *said* they would be there for you, are, in fact, not there for you. They're nowhere to be found. No calls, no texts, no one showing up to help—only radio silence.

It's a secondary loss that you don't see coming. It's yet another gut punch.

It adds to the isolation, the loneliness.

In the most difficult time of life, it becomes necessary to let relationships come to a close. And as for the people still present in your life, it becomes necessary to let them be wrong about you.

Journal Prompt

Which relationships have faded or ended since your loss? How does that feel?

What would it look like to gently release someone who cannot meet you where you are?

Why You Need Grief-Savvy People

In the most difficult time of life, it's crucial that you find your new people.

The ones who get it. Who have walked the journey themselves. The grief-savvy people who know how to sit next to you in your pain. Who don't try to fix you. Who don't attempt to rush you, or tell you to look on the bright side, or offer you platitudes.

The people who never start a sentence with, "At least...." As in "At least you have your siblings."

The people who aren't competing in the grief Olympics, comparing your loss to their own, saying, "It's just like when....."

Find your people who see you exactly as you are. The people who can sit with pain and not feel in any way uncomfortable. Find your people who will cheer you on in your smallest of victories. The people who don't try to find the "right" words, because they know that words often fail.

A group of grief-savvy people can make all the difference in your healing.

You'll have the connection and community you crave. That will help you avoid the isolation so common after the loss of a spouse.

Grief-savvy people can become a source of deep, authentic connections that can last a lifetime.

You can tap the collective wisdom of the group, and share and contribute to others.

You'll put less pressure on those who genuinely don't get it (good for them) and less pressure on yourself to try to help them understand (because, after all, they can't possibly understand).

You'll feel seen, understood, and validated.

We humans aren't meant to be alone. Not only does the loss of our person make us feel deeply alone, but the loss of other connections adds significantly to the burden.

I urge you to find your new, grief-savvy people. Don't wait.

Journal Prompt

When has someone said or done something that made you feel unseen or misunderstood?

What has someone said or done that made you feel deeply understood?

What qualities do you need most in the people who surround you now?

How do you feel when you imagine being with people who truly "get it"?

Where to Find Grief-Savvy People

Now, your brain will tell you that it's too hard. That you don't have the energy. That you're too introverted, too busy, or too exhausted. And those seem so true.

But what if they're not true? What if connecting with grief-savvy people is actually not hard? What if it's not hard even if you're an introvert, busy, or tired?

Grief groups exist throughout the United States, both virtually and in person. GriefShare (www.griefshare.org), a Christian group program, is just one example.

Many hospitals and hospice agencies offer grief support. Groups like these may help you for a time, and you'll meet other people who are also walking through a grief journey of some type.

Soaring Spirits International (www.soaringspirits.org) offers many wonderful programs exclusively for those who have lost a spouse. One of these is Regional Social Groups, which happen across the U.S., both virtually and in person.

Soaring Spirits also offers Camp Widow, a conference for widowed people, which is a source of connection, understanding and learning and has marked the beginning of life-long, deep friendships. (No actual camping is involved.)

MeetUp.com is another way to connect with people in your area. You may find a grief group or a group specifically for widowed people. Whatever your interests, MeetUp likely has a group. It's designed to bring people together, to welcome newcomers, to create connections.

Journal Prompt

What's one step you could take this week to explore a group or connection that might help you?

What story is your brain telling you about why it's "too hard" to seek out new people—and is it true?

Wonderful, supportive friendships are made in each of these settings.

I started a group for widowed people in 2020. It began with one member. Today there are 150 members. We are friends. We support each other. We laugh and we cry. We go on walks, we share meals, we karaoke, we dance, and we genuinely enjoy being together.

We have extroverts and introverts. Some are new to this journey; others are veterans. Every age group is represented. All feel welcome.

What brings me joy is seeing the sense of belonging. The friendships that form. The familiarity and authenticity that comes so naturally to a group of widowed people.

And although this is not the purpose of the group, two of the members got married, mentioning their late spouses in their wedding vows.

Although everyone's journey is unique, there is a level of understanding that goes without saying.

The Gift of Understanding

And that's what I hope for you: that you'll find a few grief savvy people who get it, who get you. Who accurately see your whereabouts, who will choose to keep you company in exactly that place.

People who will walk alongside you as you learn this version of yourself, and as you continue to grow. Who want to hear about your person. Who want to help you honor your person.

You deserve that.

———————◆———————

Journal Prompt

Who in your life right now feels like "your people"?

How can you nurture those relationships while staying open to finding new ones?

———————◆———————

NINE

Guilt, Regret, and Anger

When Guilt Feels Overwhelming

I n the early years after my husband's passing, I was filled with what I called guilt, and yet I couldn't find a single resource to help me.

Every book I read started with a sterile, textbook summary of the Five Stages of Grief, which launched me from guilt to anger—partly because the Five Stages of Grief were never meant for people grieving a loss, partly because they're decades old and outdated, and in large part because grief felt anything but categorical, linear, or organized.

Across the room the book would sail.

No matter how long ago your person passed, it's likely that you have felt guilt. Like all feelings, it comes from thoughts.

- "I should have been able to save him."
- "I should have seen the signs."
- "I gave him a 'fatal' dose of his home hospice medications."

- "I should have been at his bedside."
- "I should have convinced him to see a doctor."
- "I shouldn't have let him go to the doctor appointments without me."
- "I should have diagnosed it sooner."
- "I should have made her fight harder."
- "I shouldn't have encouraged him to get so much treatment."
- "I shouldn't have been so optimistic."

Or some other such way you believe you did it "wrong." I've rarely met anyone who thinks they did it "right."

Journal Prompt

What specific "should" thoughts do you notice yourself replaying?

How do these thoughts make you feel in your body?

Well-Practiced Thoughts Become Beliefs

The more you think thoughts like these, the more you believe them, and the sooner the brain files these beliefs away in the subconscious mind—which makes them harder to find.

Yet all thoughts, conscious and subconscious, cause feelings, which drive actions, which create results.

So while you may no longer be thinking the thought, word for word, in your brain, you may notice a feeling of guilt, or you may notice yourself taking actions (or not taking actions) because of guilt.

Perhaps you don't allow yourself to fully experience happiness or joy, given that your person is dead, and to some degree, you hold yourself responsible for doing it "wrong."

Maybe you can only give yourself permission to live a metered, mediocre life because you didn't keep your person alive.

These guilt-producing thoughts have no timestamp. Left unexamined, they will live in your brain forever more. (See Chapter 21, Brain Tendencies, specifically the section called "Confirmation Bias.")

Journal Prompt

What do you believe you "did wrong"?

If a close friend were telling you this, how would you respond to them?

My Self-Imposed Prison Sentence

I lived with guilt for years. It was solitary confinement in a prison of my own creation. My brain chose it, in fact, as many brains do.

As we learned in Chapter 2, it's called counterfactual thinking. In the moments when you daydream about alternate, remarkably better outcomes, you have a sense of control: "If only X, then Y," where Y is that your person lived.

The brain loves a sense of control because it feels safer, and especially given that your world has spun out of control. Adding to that, when we're not living in the dreamland of counterfactual thinking, then we're being gut punched with the reality of this life, our person's physical absence, and all of what that means.

Journal Prompt

What "if only" thoughts come up most often for you?

How might these thoughts be your brain's way of reaching for control?

Sketchy Trench-Coat Guy

For me, feeling guilty was a bit like walking down a busy street, and in some dark alley, there was a man in a black trench coat calling to me. For years, I would stop, go to him, and have a lengthy conversation about how I failed, how I missed the signs, and how I should have been able to save my husband. The "evidence" was everywhere.

If you can relate to this, here are some important things to know.

Guilt Is Different from Regret

Guilt and regret are different, and it's more than semantics. Guilt is when a jury would find you guilty. You had all the facts, and you knew the "right" thing to do, but you chose to do the "wrong" thing instead.

Regret is when you had whatever facts you had at the time and made a decision based on what you thought was best.

Journal Prompt

Looking back, which of your experiences are actually regret — not guilt?

How does it feel different when you reframe guilt as regret?

Hindsight Is 20/20

It's tempting to Monday Morning Quarterback our former selves. It's easy to sit here with all the facts and knowing the outcome, and criticize the past version of you who had only partial facts, who was navigating the worst-case scenario of life, and who did your best given what you knew at the time.

When I looked at the situation honestly, what I actually felt was regret. Knowing that took the sting out. Later, I realized that even regret was optional (it, too, was a product of my own thinking) and that became my next exercise in mental flexibility. I tried to build an argument for Debate Team B (remember them from Chapter 6?).

- What if I wasn't supposed to save him?
- What if he wasn't save-able?
- What if he wasn't for me to save?
- Who do I think I am, that I am so powerful that I can determine life and death?

Do I wish I could have saved him? Absolutely, yes. Do I continue to hold myself responsible for not saving him? No, I took that rock out of my purse.

Do I still carry a heavy purse? Yes, but it isn't one ounce heavier than absolutely necessary.

I still occasionally bump into Trench-Coat Guy in my mind. I see him out of the corner of my eye, and I know he's calling to me, but I simply keep walking. "Not today," I tell him. "Not today."

Journal Prompt

What does your "Trench Coat Guy" look like?

What does he whisper to you?

How might you anticipate him and keep walking past him instead of engaging?

Anger Is Common, Normal, and *Optional*

Like regret, anger is a common feeling after losing a spouse.

Anger at your spouse for:

- Leaving you to deal with so many things.
- Ending their life.
- Not being proactive with his health.
- Not advocating enough in the healthcare system.

Or maybe you're angry at life for the hand it dealt you.

Or angry at the person who ended your spouse's life.

Or angry at God.

Or angry with yourself.

Or just plain angry at everything.

Anger is a feeling that the brain actually chooses because anger feels less terrible than the pain of your loss.

My client Lora told me that she was ready to stop feeling anger toward the person who inadvertently ended Lora's husband's life. I asked her to tell me all the reasons she was angry at him. We wrote all those thoughts on paper.

Then, we explored other thoughts on the topic that created feelings other than anger. Lora then spent the following week trying various thoughts on for size, noticing how true they felt to her, and what feelings they prompted.

The next week she came to our session and said, "If I don't feel anger, then I feel the pain of the loss, and that pain feels harder."

That's the thing about anger. To the brain, it feels less terrible. The brain is hardwired to feel good; in absence of good, then "less terrible" will do.

We worked together to help her process the pain (see Chapter 4) and she intentionally chose true thoughts that caused feelings other than anger. It wasn't an overnight process, but it was worth it.

Journal Prompt

Who or what are you angry at right now? List every reason.

How does anger feel in your body? How does it affect your day-to-day life?

Working With Anger

If you feel anger, it's okay. It's normal. You get to feel anger as long as you want, and I'm not trying to rush you out of it. But when you feel ready, write down all the reasons you're angry. Acknowledge them. Notice how each makes you feel.

Then, brainstorm what Debate Team B might say. Could the opposite possibly be true? What else is true? Your brain is hard wired for efficiency, so it won't want to exert this effort—but you can direct it nonetheless. You're not committing to anything, but simply thought shopping. You're trying on thoughts for size, noticing how they feel. That's all. You're flexing your mental flexibility muscles. As you shop, you're looking for thoughts that are true, useful, and kind.

In terms of truth, on a scale of 1 to 10, where 10 indicates strong belief, how would you rate the thoughts that come up in your brainstorm? Aim for a 6 or higher.

In terms of usefulness, notice how each thought makes you feel. Guilt, regret, and anger are not useful feelings, so keep shopping until you notice other feelings that are more useful and comfortable. The good news is that thoughts are infinite, and thought shopping is free.

In terms of kindness, ask yourself if you would say this to someone you love. You'll know immediately if the thought is kind. Remember, love is the way forward. Loving yourself is the most direct path.

Journal Prompt

What other thoughts could you try on (Debate Team B)?

Which of these thoughts feel true, useful, and kind?

On a scale of 1–10, how true does the new thought you're trying feel?

What feeling does it create in you?

Would you say this thought to someone you love?

If yes, can you say it to yourself?

———————◆———————

TEN

Forgiveness

F ew words carry as much weight—or trigger as much resistance—
as forgiveness. For many widowed people, it feels impossible,
unfair, or even offensive to suggest it. After all, how could anyone expect
you to "forgive" when you're living with the fallout of profound loss,
broken promises, careless words, or even betrayals that surfaced after
your spouse's death? Forgiveness can feel like trying to chip away at a
glacier with an icepick: exhausting, hopeless, and pointless.

And yet, what if forgiveness is actually not a monumental, drawn-out struggle? What if it didn't depend on apologies, reconciliation, or condoning
anyone's behavior? In this chapter, I'll offer a fresh and practical way to
think about forgiveness—one that puts the power back in your hands. Not
as a gift you give to someone else, but as a release you offer yourself.

The Weight of Anger and Resentment

It's natural and common for widowed people to feel anger and resentment—about the nature of the loss, the behavior of family or friends, the

absence of those who said they would be there, the unhelpful comments, the weirdos who suddenly resurface, the predatory tactics of scammers, the discovery of infidelity, and so much more.

Journal Prompt

When you hear the word "forgiveness," what emotions or thoughts come up for you?

Does it feel heavy, impossible, or unfair? Write down the first words that surface.

I've gone to church all my life, and have always thought of forgiveness as a long, slow, difficult process. But when I discovered the tools of coaching, the following definition, and path to forgiveness, everything changed for me.

First, we must unlearn what we think we know.

What Forgiveness Is (and Isn't)

It's easy to confuse forgiveness with condoning someone's behavior or accepting an apology—which can be tough pills to swallow.

But in truth, it is neither of those things.

Forgiveness is simply deciding to stop feeling angry and resentful. That's it.

You're ready to forgive when you make the decision to stop feeling angry and resentful. That's all forgiveness is: to set down anger and resentment.

As for how to do it, I outline the few surprisingly simple steps below, which all happen inside of your own brain. To be clear, forgiveness does not require:

- Having a conversation with the other person
- Telling them that you've forgiven them
- Accepting an apology from someone
- Allowing someone back into your life
- Condoning behavior

Those actions are all optional when it comes to forgiveness—optional, not mandatory.

Journal Prompt

Who or what do you feel pressure to forgive, and why?

How have you confused forgiveness with condoning, excusing, or reconciling in the past?

The Freedom of Forgiveness

Forgiveness is truly an inside job. The only person who needs to know that you've forgiven someone is you. Forgiveness is just another name for freedom: freedom from anger and resentment.

American author Jonathan Lockwood Huie is quoted as saying, "Forgive others, not because they deserve forgiveness, but because you deserve peace."

When is the right time to forgive? Only you can decide when you want to stop feeling anger and resentment. Sometimes we just want to feel those feelings, and that's okay. Other times, we realize that anger and resentment are heavy and feel terrible. They're like carrying rocks in your purse.

Journal Prompt

Imagine setting down anger and resentment like taking rocks out of a heavy bag. How would that change your day-to-day experience?

What kind of peace might you gain if you chose forgiveness for yourself?

Anger and resentment are also an inside job. Meaning that the other person doesn't experience your anger and resentment—only you do.

Your anger and resentment don't punish the other person. They punish only you.

As the old saying goes, withholding forgiveness is like drinking poison and waiting for the other person to get sick.

A powerful question to ask yourself is whether you want to continue to feel anger and resentment, or if you are ready to shed those feelings. You always have the choice to shed those feelings, and if you want to, you can make that choice today.

First, let's understand why we feel anger and resentment.

Why Anger and Resentment Linger

The person's words or actions happened, or maybe it was their silence or inactions. Then we have a thought about their words, actions, or inactions. That thought creates how we feel. We feel anger and resentment because of what we're thinking about the person and their behavior.

To us, our thoughts seem absolutely true. But they're not serving us because they create anger and resentment.

While the person's words or actions are outside of your control, your thoughts about them are completely within your control. This means that the person actually has no power over you. Your power is in your thinking.

Journal Prompt

In what ways have you believed someone else still has power over you because of what they did—or didn't do?

How does it shift things to realize that your thoughts—not their actions—determine how you feel today?

How to Forgive in 3 Steps

1. **Consider the person's words, actions or inactions, and write down all the thoughts you have about them.** Notice that these thoughts create anger and resentment.
2. **Next, ask your brain to consider what other thoughts might also be true.** Now, your brain won't want to do this work because it's already committed to the current thoughts and is

certain that they're true. Simply ask your brain to imagine other possibilities. There are no right or wrong answers. Just make a list. Here are some possibilities to consider:

   a. Hurt people sometimes hurt people.

   b. They did the best they could given what they knew at the time.

   c. Just because they don't love me the way I would like doesn't mean that they don't love me with all they have.

   d. It was always supposed to happen this way.

   e. It was painful, and yet it shaped me into who I am today.

3. **Review your list of new thoughts.** Try each thought on like you would an outfit. Notice how each makes you feel. Pick the thoughts that feel true and that create a feeling that you want to feel, one that feels better than anger or resentment.

To quote British author Alain de Botton, "Forgiveness requires a sense that bad behavior is a sign of suffering rather than malice."

Journal Prompt

Write down all the thoughts you have about someone you have not forgiven. Notice which ones fuel anger or resentment.

What alternative thoughts might also be true? Try listing at least three.

Which of those new thoughts helps you feel even a little lighter?

When Resentment Turns into Compassion

Years after my husband's death, I realized that I was still carrying anger and resentment toward someone who hurt him deeply and repeatedly. I was locked in a thought loop, thinking that it should have never happened, and he deserved better. It was only when I got curious that I was able choose other thinking. I asked myself, "But why would a person behave that way?" And with each answer, I asked, "But why?" again and again.

I was eventually able to decide that the person who hurt him was struggling, deeply insecure, and unhappy. That thought made me feel compassion. I wasn't necessarily aiming for compassion, but I ended up there.

Journal Prompt

Think of a person whose behavior hurt you deeply. Ask yourself: Why might they have acted that way? Keep asking, "Why?" until you reach a place of deeper understanding.

What shifts when you consider their actions as coming from suffering rather than malice?

Now, brains are creatures of habit. Your brain will likely still offer you those well-practiced thoughts of the past, and you'll then feel anger and resentment creep back into your body. That's to be expected. This is your chance to redirect your brain toward the new thoughts that you created and tested in Step 3 above.

With practice, these new thoughts will become your default thinking.

Welcome to the freedom of forgiveness.

Forgiving Yourself

Now, what about you? In what ways have you not yet forgiven yourself?

We've already talked about how easy it is to Monday Morning Quarterback ourselves, to hold our past self accountable for what we didn't know, and for what we didn't know to do. We may criticize the decisions that we made with partial knowledge, the skills we had at the time, and how we functioned in the midst of a tidal wave of catastrophe unfolding, not knowing the outcome.

It's not fair. We wouldn't do that to another person. Yet your brain might lead you down this path. And when it does, remember the pledge you signed in Chapter 1. Think of the gentle and wise words of Maya Angelou: "Forgive yourself for not knowing what you didn't know before you learned it."

Journal Prompt

Write down the ways you are still blaming yourself after your spouse's death. Be specific.

What do you know now that you didn't know then?

If your spouse could speak to you today, what would they want for you?

If the anger and resentment you feel toward yourself feels extra heavy and you're ready to set it down, follow the three steps to forgiveness above. Find true to you thoughts that create any feelings other than anger and resentment. Keep trying thoughts on for size, noticing how each feels in your body.

I told myself that I should have been able to save my husband. I was well trained in CPR, and I should have seen the signs. I couldn't allow myself to live fully, because I wasn't able to save him, and I couldn't forgive myself for that. I lived in the solitary confinement of that prison of my own creation for years.

Choosing to Live Again

If the shoe were on the other foot, I would not want my husband to stop living because I did. One heart stopped beating that day, not two.

The other heart kept beating, but opted out of truly living—until I was willing to explore other thoughts, other possibilities. I was giving myself so much power, as if I had the power to save him.

I did this to myself even though my experience in acute care cardiology, specifically in the cardiac cath lab, told me that some people simply cannot be saved.

My intentional thought is, "I was not capable of saving him, because he wasn't for me to save."

If I was meant to save him, I would have saved him. While I wish it weren't the case, there is no upside to arguing with reality or keeping myself locked away, serving a life sentence unnecessarily. (We'll talk more about arguing with reality in Chapter 11.)

I now choose to think that the degree to which I build a big, differently beautiful life, I honor him. The degree to which I achieve my potential in this life, I honor him.

I won't waste any additional heartbeats opting out of this life I'm still living. I choose to forgive myself, and I choose to live fully. I hope you will, too.

Journal Prompt

What new intentional thought could you choose that helps you feel lighter, freer, or more at peace?

How can living fully become an act of honoring your spouse's life and love?

ELEVEN

Acceptance Redefined: Releasing the Argument with Reality

No matter how long ago your spouse passed, you may struggle with this new reality that you didn't sign up for. It doesn't seem real. It can be incredibly hard to accept. In this chapter, I offer a fresh perspective on acceptance, and lack thereof.

A Brain in Confusion

First, it's important to recognize that the brain genuinely doesn't understand what's happened. Remember how we talked about it being experiences over time, not time itself, that changes things? (See Chapter 2 for a review.)

Of course, you know that your person died.

But you've spent years, maybe decades with your person. Your brain understands the world with their physical presence in it. It now needs to rewire itself, and that takes new lived experiences that happen over time —often over months and even years.

In the meantime, your brain is genuinely confused.

Journal Prompt

In what ways do you still expect your spouse to still be physically present?

How does it feel to notice yourself expecting what logically can't happen?

Remember the pledge you signed in Chapter 1? The best way to support yourself is to know that your brain is adjusting to this new reality. Know that it's completely normal to anticipate them coming home, even though you know they died. Be patient with your grieving brain. Remind yourself, lovingly, that rewiring requires new lived experiences, and that takes time.

Please don't kick yourself when this happens. You simply have a normal human brain trying to understand that the unthinkable has happened. Be gentle with yourself.

Journal Prompt

How can you remind yourself gently that this is your brain's way of trying to adjust, not a sign that something is wrong with you?

In addition to the genuine confusion you experience after loss, the brain offers thoughts that I would call arguing with reality.

When the Brain Argues with Reality

It often sounds like: "This shouldn't have happened to him, to us," or "He should be here."

These are sentences that your brain offers, and they seem so very true. It's completely normal to have thoughts like these, and there's nothing at all wrong with it.

But they feel extra terrible. Arguing with reality always feels extra terrible. And anytime there's a chance to feel less terrible, I want you to know about it.

Because the journey is hard enough already. It doesn't have to be one ounce harder than necessary.

So, be "on to" your brain. Notice when it offers thoughts that argue with reality. Notice how they make you feel. Notice your energy levels draining.

Decide if you want to continue to think these thoughts. It's okay if you do. Maybe you want to give yourself a time limit to do so.

Or perhaps you want to practice acceptance.

Journal Prompt

What are the "should" or "shouldn't" statements your brain often repeats about your loss?

How do you feel in your body when you think these thoughts? Do they drain your energy or add to your suffering?

Redefining Acceptance

Let's define acceptance. It's a tricky word. We tend to make it mean more than it actually does.

Acceptance is simply saying, "this happened."

When we accept something, we acknowledge that it factually happened.

Acceptance does not mean that you condone what happened. Or that you would have chosen it. Or that you're letting people off the hook in any way.

It simply means that it happened, in exactly the way it did.

Acceptance is syncing up with the reality of the situation, at least for a moment.

Journal Prompt

How does it feel to think of acceptance as simply "this happened," without adding anything more to it?

Choosing Acceptance, Moment by Moment

If you choose acceptance for yourself, you will suffer less. You'll lighten the load you carry. It's a milestone moment in the journey.

You will still have moments of genuine confusion about your reality. You will still have thoughts that argue with reality, too. Both are normal.

Journal Prompt

What thoughts or practices help you touch—even briefly—the reality of this happened?

How does it feel when you let go of arguing with reality, even for a moment?

Be patient with your brain as it learns to understand the world anew.

Be patient with your brain as it offers a wide variety of thoughts that argue with reality, and then gently redirect it, if you choose, toward syncing up with your current reality.

Do this for no other reason than to feel a little better, to have a little extra energy for things that matter most to you.

Journal Prompt

If acceptance could give you just a little more energy for something that matters to you, what would you want to use that energy for?

When your brain resists reality or gets confused, how can you respond to yourself with gentleness instead of judgment?

What reminder could you keep close by (a phrase or image) that helps you be patient with your brain's rewiring process?

TWELVE

Learning to Decide Again

When Decisiveness Disappears

Decisions used to be second nature. You knew what you liked, what you wanted, and how to get it done. But after loss, even the smallest choices can feel impossible. Should you buy the coffee mugs? Say yes to the invitation? Keep wearing your ring? Every decision feels weighted with meaning, as if there's a "right" and "wrong" way to live without your person. What once felt effortless now feels exhausting, and many widowed people describe a kind of decision paralysis that drains their energy and leaves them doubting themselves at every turn.

Journal Prompt

When was the last time you felt stuck in making a decision?

What made it feel so difficult?

The Loss of Shared Decision-Making

Many people relied on, or collaborated with, their person to make decisions as a couple. One of the many perks of life before loss is making shared decisions: having a dialogue with your life partner, analyzing the pros and cons together, then making a mutual choice and ultimately sharing ownership of the outcome, for better or worse. Relying on one another's strength, knowledge, and experience brings a level of comfort to the decision-making process. Generally, making mutual decisions means that you have each other's back, no matter the outcome. It feels safe.

Journal Prompt

In what ways did you and your spouse share the responsibility of decision-making?

What do you miss most about that partnership?

No matter if you were once decisive, collaborative, or even dependent on your spouse for decision-making, here's what I want you to know: You're not supposed to be good at it now. You're not supposed to know how to do it. Everything changed, including you and your brain.

Most widowed people have heard the adage, "Don't make any big decisions in the first year." There is some truth to that advice, but the actual experience of losing one's spouse means facing a relentless series of decisions. For some, the decisions start at the hospital, then the funeral home, and they seemingly never end. After the first wave of decisions come many more. Sell the house? Clean his closet? Wear the wedding ring? Get an alarm system? Say yes to a lunch invitation? Go on the trip?

Why Every Choice Feels So Heavy

We must rely solely on ourselves to make these choices, precisely when we are at our very worst, and just when we need our spouse the most. Enter decision fatigue—that exhausted feeling you get when struggling to make a decision. Decision fatigue is draining on a good day, and in life after loss it zaps whatever energy is left. The primitive brain is immersed in fear and scarcity, and from that place it suggests that there is always a right and a wrong decision, and that decisions are irreversible and urgent.

Yet often none of that is true.

Journal Prompt

Which current decisions feel most urgent to you?

What would happen if you gave yourself more time?

Think of a decision you're facing now: Is it truly irreversible, or might you have room to adjust later?

What options beyond "Yes" and "No" might you not be seeing?

Questions to Lighten the Load

When you are struggling with a decision, ask yourself the following questions:

1. **When does this decision absolutely need be made?** Your brain may be suggesting that everything is urgent, when in reality some decisions can be made later—sometimes much later.

2. **Is this decision reversible?** I remember thinking about whether I wanted to take off my wedding ring or not. It seemed like this was an irreversible decision. Which is kind of funny because it just isn't. (And if you're wondering, I decided not to take it off for years, and I still wear it today whenever I want).

3. **Are there more than just two options?** Our brains love the simplicity of two options, black or white, safety or danger. But very often there are many other options that we don't readily see, unless we look. (See Chapter 21, and specifically the section on "Absolute Thinking.")

4. **List your reasons you would decide yes, and list your reasons you would decide no.** Which reasons do you like the most? Notice where there is fear and/or scarcity.

5. **Consider that there is no "good" or "bad" decision.** Notice that there is a pro and con for any decision you make. When you make a decision, you're simply choosing one set of pros and cons over another.

6. **If your person were here,** given the current circumstances, what would he/she say?

7. **Fast forward to a future version of you who has what you currently want for yourself.** How would she advise you about the current decision? What moves you toward who you want to be?

Give yourself a timeline to decide. Indecision feels terrible, so it's better that you decide, one way or the other. Your brain will want to avoid the discomfort of making a decision. Ask yourself what is on the other side of that discomfort. What is the best- and worst-case scenario? And what if the worst-case scenario is missing out on the best-case scenario?

Journal Prompt

Imagine your future self, who is living the life you hope to create. What advice would Future You give about this decision?

When you look at your reasons for yes and for no, which ones come from fear, and which come from hope?

Deciding to Have Your Own Back

Using these considerations, you will carefully examine your options, and make your decision. Then, make one more important decision: that your choice is the right one for you. In other words the most important decision is the decision to have your own back. To echo Maya Angelou's wise words, quoted in Chapter 1, be on your own side.

Journal Prompt

How can you practice "having your own back" with the decision you make today?

THIRTEEN

Goals: Moving Toward What You Want

I t's okay if you dislike the word "goal." Maybe that was once associated with climbing the corporate ladder, and the last thing you want in life after loss is to have a goal. I get it. Call it an Area of Focus, or Next Hard Thing, or insert any other word or phrase that works for you.

No matter what you call it, the reality is that some things we must accomplish, and other things we want to accomplish, big and small.

If you're navigating your first year of loss, your goals will likely be different from in your fifth year, or tenth year. Regardless, this chapter offers fresh insight about goals, which applies to grief and life in general.

But First, a Battery Check

As a precursor to goal setting, it's important to check your energy levels (see Chapter 7). If your batteries are drained, then self-care is the most important goal for now. A little self-care goes a long way in enabling you to accomplish goals, but self-care is the starting point. If your battery packs are drained, recharge them first so you have the energy to set your sights on goals.

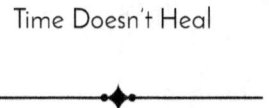

Journal Prompt

How charged are your battery packs: brain, body and spirit? (low, medium, high)

If your "batteries" are drained, what's one small act of self-care you can choose today to recharge?

Three Versions of You

In thinking about goals, it's helpful to consider three versions of yourself: your past self, your future self, and your present self.

When **your past self** came up with a goal, you were using your prefrontal cortex to do so. That's the part of the brain that makes long-term plans. It knows what would be good for you, and makes plans accordingly.

The **future version of you** has already accomplished the goal. She's enjoying the fruits of her labor. She's grateful to the past version of her who set the goal, and then took the steps to make it happen.

The **present version of you** is likely operating with her primitive brain, which only focuses on the here and now. This is the part of the brain that wants immediate gratification, seeks to avoid discomfort and find pleasure instead, and always aims to be efficient.

This explains why your current self couldn't care less about any goal. How about ice cream instead? While sitting on the couch, binging your new favorite series.

Avoid the discomfort of striving for a goal? *Check.*

Seek the pleasure of ice cream instead? *Check.*

While lying on the couch, conserving energy? *Check and check.*

Journal Prompt

What is one goal your past self wanted for you?

If you imagine your future self who has already reached this goal, what advice would Future You give Present You right now?

How is Present You resisting the goal? What does your primitive brain want instead?

Don't Make It Mean You're Failing

This is where it can be easy for self-criticism to roll in. It's easy to kick yourself, ridicule yourself, or deem yourself a failure. None of which helps, and all of which actually keeps you stuck in a spin cycle of inaction.

You're not lazy, broken, or failing. You simply have a primitive brain that's doing its job: living in the moment, seeking pleasure, avoiding pain, being efficient.

If you're a high achiever, you're thinking, "I get that, but I never had this problem before." Remember, your person's death changed you, too. It changed how your brain is working. The primitive part of your brain is on overdrive, and it's very likely the loudest voice in the room, louder than ever before.

Journal Prompt

When have you recently criticized yourself for not following through?

What happens if you view that moment with compassion instead of judgment?

As you know from Chapter 2, grief hits hard, impacting brain and body, leaving nothing untouched. Your energy levels are miniscule. Your primitive brain has a strong argument for opting out of the goal. It makes sense. If you can approach it from this place of understanding, then you can make an important shift.

Talk to Yourself More Than You Listen to Yourself

Intentional self-talk engages your prefrontal cortex. Which is to say, talk to yourself more than you listen to yourself. Remind yourself why Past You set this goal; review all the reasons. Then, fast forward to Future You who is enjoying the benefits of having accomplished this goal. What advice would Future You offer to Present You?

Sometimes you're truly drained and you need to focus on self-care. And a lot of the time, you can take some small action toward a well-established goal. You have enough energy to cast a vote for your future self, to set Future You up for success.

You likely already have a to-do list a mile long. I'd also encourage you to create a want-to-do list. Doing things you actually want to do is helpful. It sends some feel-good hormones into your system. It's a break from the have-to drudgery. It keeps your must-dos and your want-tos in balance.

Which means you'll need to ask yourself an important question: What do you want?

Journal Prompt

What's on your "must-do" list today?

What's one thing you'd love to put on a "want-to-do" list?

How would including more "want-tos" shift your energy?

Want List

Make a list of 25 things you want. You can include things you already have and still want. For me, I have a home and I love my home and I want to keep my home, so my home would be on my want list. The same goes for my vehicle. Also include things you want, but don't yet have. Set your brain free to brainstorm, explore, and dream, come up with "crazy" ideas. Don't filter anything out; write down everything that comes to mind.

Journal Prompt

What do you truly want right now, big or small?

Create a Measurable Goal

Once you have your list of at least 25 items, pick one as your goal.

Next, let's put the goal into a measurable sentence. It must be measurable so you'll know when you've completed it. Select a deadline. Pick something that causes you to stretch, but that you can complete within the time frame you chose and in the time you have available to you. For example, "By October 23, I will have canceled three streaming subscriptions and start using the Calm app daily instead."

Journal Prompt

Write your goal in a measurable way (so you'll know when it's done).

Your Compelling "Why"

Then, write down all the reasons why you want to achieve this goal. They don't necessarily need to be deep. Write down every reason you can think of.

Journal Prompt

What are all of your compelling "Why?"s for wanting this?

Actions

Next, write every action you need to take to accomplish this goal. Break each action down into smaller steps as needed.

Journal Prompt

What are all the steps to achieve this goal?

Obstacles and Strategies

There will be obstacles to achieving your goal, and that's the way of it. List all the obstacles you might encounter. For each obstacle, identify a strategy or skill you'll use to overcome the obstacle.

Let's say your goal is to gain 3 pounds of muscle in the next 3 months. You'll use a body composition scale to measure your results. Your compelling why is to reverse osteopenia and to prevent becoming frail and falling. Plus, you'd like to move through your day-to-day life with more ease and play on the floor with grandkids.

You created a list of actions, the first of which was to find a nearby gym with strength training classes. You also decided you'll need to purchase quality shoes, get the class schedule, and drive to the class.

One obstacle you can foresee is fitting this class into your schedule, which can get busy with appointments, volunteering, and social gatherings. You then devise a strategy for this obstacle, which is to attend the earliest class, 3 days a week, and treat it with the importance of a doctor's appointment.

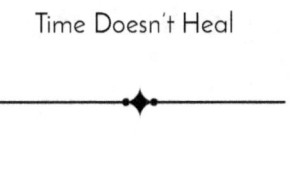

Journal Prompt

What obstacles might you face?

What strategies could you use to overcome those obstacles?

Make a Plan

Now, take your actions list and sort them in the order of execution. Make them as clear and specific as possible. Determine how much time each action will take. Add each item to your calendar with the time frames you've decided on.

Expect Resistance

When it's time to follow your calendar, expect your primitive brain to have "better" ideas. In the moment, you probably won't feel like it. Anticipate this, and then when it happens, you'll be much less likely to make it mean that you're failing. You can simply thank your primitive brain for doing its job. Then, review your compelling "Why?"s, fast forward to your future self and get advice, and then take the immediate next step on your calendar.

In our muscle-building example, you might lay out your gym clothes and shoes the night before, set your alarm, and have your pre-workout meal prepped in advance. Even so, you might not feel like going, and that's when you can leverage the power of feelings.

Journal Prompt

When your primitive brain doesn't want to follow through, how will you talk to yourself?

Useful Feelings

Chapter 3 explained that thoughts cause feelings, and feelings drive action. Working toward your goal means taking action, so it's logical to find a feeling that will inspire the actions you want to take.

For many people, motivation comes to mind, but motivation is only a spark. It's not a good idea to wait to feel motivated, because motivation wanes. Other feelings are more useful as you work toward a goal. "Intentional," "deliberate," and "dedicated" are some of my favorites. They don't necessarily feel as good as motivation does, but they are more reliable and get the job done in the long term.

You may have a feeling that would naturally drive the actions you want to take toward your goal, and a true thought you could choose that would naturally create that feeling in your body. Experiment with different thoughts and feelings to see what is most helpful as you work toward your goal.

Journal Prompt

Which feeling do you want to drive your actions: intentional, deliberate, dedicated—or another?

What thought could you practice to create that feeling in your body?

It's the Thought That Counts

The single thought that drives the actions I take in my work as a coach for widowed people is, "People are hurting, and I can help them." That thought makes me feel intentionality, which naturally drives a wide variety of actions such as creating my next podcast episode, delivering a presentation, preparing for a webinar, and drafting an email.

I don't have to force myself to do any of that. I don't have to get tough on myself, or muscle my way through the day. I simply think that true thought, feel the feeling, and I'm off to the races.

Journal Prompt

List some true and useful thoughts to help you achieve your goal.

It's About Who You Become

Achieving a goal, however small, is a big win in life after loss. But what's more important than what you achieve is who you become in the process. You will restore confidence and build a foundation of self-trust and capability.

But that doesn't happen only when a goal is accomplished. Each time you take an action toward a goal, you build integrity with yourself. You willingly choose to feel the discomfort associated with the action. You step, ever so slightly, into the zone of unfamiliarity.

Growth and Comfort Do Not Coexist

And each step is an acknowledgment that growth and comfort do not coexist. It's a refusal to opt out of life, a rejection of the mundane, mediocre existence that is available to you. You're choosing instead to move toward your untapped potential, to your life at full capacity, because you're alive and because life is worth truly living.

In the words of Dr. Martin Luther King, Jr., "You don't have to see the whole staircase, just take the first step."

Journal Prompt

Who are you becoming as you take steps toward your goal?

How does each action (even small ones) rebuild trust in yourself?

What part of you is growing stronger as you step into discomfort?

FOURTEEN

Confidence After Loss

The first lesson in judo is how to fall. If you aren't afraid to fall, you can commit yourself 100% to anything you do.

Perhaps you've never trained in judo, but you have fallen—and hard.

Life dealt you the biggest blow, and it reverberated throughout your body and your whole existence, leaving nothing unscathed. It left you uncertain if you could keep living, and wondering if you even wanted to.

And here you are, showing up for another day. Putting one foot in front of the other. Reading this book and believing that there's more for you.

You've survived your darkest days. It hasn't been pretty, nor linear, nor categorical. There were no boxes to check, no rulebook to follow. It's a gritty, messy, unpredictable way forward, and you keep showing up for it.

When the worst has happened, and you've survived, you have a comparative value that can be incredibly useful. You can commit yourself 100% to anything you choose for yourself.

Who You've Become

Often as widowed people, we want to know the "how." We'd love someone to tell us the steps forward. But what matters more than the "how" is the "who."

Think about all the things you've accomplished since your person died. Those are tasks, decisions, paperwork, and the like. Make a list. This is your accomplishment list, and it should include small and large accomplishments.

Then, for each item, think about it in this way, "I'm the person who…" and then add the task you accomplished.

My personal examples include:

- I'm the person who made funeral arrangements on our wedding anniversary.
- I'm the person who planted an orchard and learned how to farm for a supplementary income.
- I'm the person who figured out how to keep our ranch.
- I'm the person who learned how to fix the broken things, lift the heavy things, and believe in herself again.

It's not about how to do something; it's about being the person who knows they can figure out a way to get it done.

Journal Prompt

Make a list of at least 10 things you've accomplished since your spouse died, big or small. Then write them as "I'm the person who…" statements.

Debate Team A vs. Debate Team B

The human brain is hard wired to keep us alive, so it's good at pointing out danger, scarcity and uncertainty. Left unattended, your brain will convince you that you don't have enough, don't know enough and that overall, you aren't cut out for this life. You find yourself standing on a shaky foundation.

As we did in Chapter 6, we'll call that Debate Team A. Fair enough, primitive brain. Noted. Thanks for doing your job.

Now, let's see what Debate Team B has to say.

Debate Team B relies on facts. Factually speaking, what *have* you done? What *have* you accomplished? What *have* you learned, fixed, and figured out?

Remember the full-time job that death requires? You did that: the decisions, arrangements, paperwork, phone calls, bills, and finances.

Journal Prompt

What factual evidence do you already have that proves you can figure things out?

Maybe you sold a house, bought a house, or helped out your family.

Maybe you got the oil changed, got new tires on the car, or called AAA when the car broke down. (I strongly believe there should be someone standing by with a trophy for accomplishing anything that is remotely proactive, like an oil change. The first one felt Herculean to me. Even as the mechanic belabored how late I was in getting it done, I didn't cry. Where's my trophy?)

You got through a bad storm and then figured out who to call to deal with the damage.

You got out of bed and faced another day, even when it felt like your life had ended.

Think about *this* version of you, and stand on that solid foundation. You're this person. Confidence starts here.

Like any feeling, confidence comes from a thought. As a starting place, I'm suggesting that you remind yourself of factually true thoughts so you can stand on a proper foundation.

Using Comparative Value

Many times in my life after loss, I've reminded myself that if I can select a casket on our wedding anniversary, I can do any other thing in this life. My friend Jeff taught me this. Widowed years prior, he treated me to dinner shortly after my loss and said, "You'll never have another bad day." At the time, I was slogging my way through tough day after long night after tough day, so I found his words confusing.

But I eventually realized he was teaching me to use my darkest days for comparative value. "Work is just work," he said. "It means nothing." "Anything you'll experience now will pale in comparison to what you've been through."

He was planting a seed, and with time, it sprouted. Sometimes I still have to gently remind myself, "This day can never be as difficult as that day. If I can do that, I can do this."

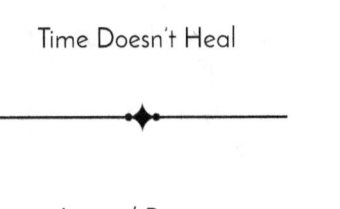

Journal Prompt

What thought can you remind yourself of when you face something hard? ("If I could ____, then I can ____.")

The River of Misery

As I write this, two clients are in the process of selling a home and buying a home. I spoke with one of them, Carol, yesterday. She said, "This feels terrible."

Carol hates where she lives. To say that it's not a fit for her is an understatement. She's excited about where she's relocating to. And yet, right now, it feels terrible.

When Carol made the offer on her new home, she jumped into the River of Misery. It's cold. And you have to swim. And the current is pushing you back toward what's familiar. It's a lot of work, and, as Carol correctly observed, it feels terrible. The River of Misery is everything the primitive brain hates, everything it's hardwired to avoid.

In fact, the primitive brain prefers familiarity so much so that it will choose a familiar misery over anything unfamiliar, including a beautiful life in another city.

Journal Prompt

Where in your life are you tempted to "settle" because it feels safer or familiar?

What new shore would you like to swim toward, even if it feels uncomfortable right now?

Building Confidence on Purpose

The primitive part of your brain will urge you to stay with what's familiar, which means it's tempting to settle. Settle for living in a place that's no longer a fit. Settle for a companion who isn't always kind. Settle for friends who no longer understand you.

John D. Rockefeller said, "Don't be afraid to give up the good to go for the great."

When a spouse dies, even the most self-confident people find their confidence shaken to the core. Anything else is rare. I would suggest that the fear will be there, but in the words of John Wayne, "Saddle up anyway."

So if you're like most, and you find yourself without an ounce of confidence, here's what to do.

1. **Make an accomplishment log** as suggested in this chapter. This offers you factual evidence that you're a person who can navigate even the darkest times.
2. **Find true to you thoughts that genuinely create confidence in your body.** Think about all the things you're confident about. Make a list.

3. **Take on a Dare of the Day practice.** What scares you just a little bit? Do that today. In doing so, you'll teach your brain that you are, in fact, safe, and you'll expand your comfort zone ever so slightly.

Journal Prompt

What is one small "Dare of the Day" you could do today to stretch yourself just a little?

What thoughts genuinely make you feel confident in your body?

Don't Settle

And when you're ready to take a bigger step, jump into the River of Misery. You'll know when the time is right.

Swim against the current toward the other shore. Your destination will either be perfect for you, or a perfect stepping stone.

When my husband died suddenly, one of the few books I found helpful was *Second Firsts,* by the lovely Christina Rasmussen. One of the most powerful lines was, "You can do the impossible because you have been through the unimaginable."

Please don't settle. A differently beautiful life is waiting for you.

Journal Prompt

In what area(s) of your life are you settling? What would it look like to choose differently?

FIFTEEN

The Limits That Live in Your Mind

 "Doubt kills more dreams than failure ever will."

—*Suzy Kassem*

When your spouse died, you were thrown into an unfamiliar life you never asked for. Every step forward has required courage in the face of fear, and often the loudest obstacles aren't external at all—they're internal.

The beliefs you hold about yourself—what you can do, what you can't do, what is or isn't possible—quietly shape your choices every day. These beliefs don't just influence how you navigate life after loss; they affect every area of your future. Whether your person died last month or decades ago, the limits you place on yourself can keep you from living fully, or you can challenge them so you grow into the capacity you still hold. This is why understanding limiting beliefs matters—not just for grief, but for life in general.

Ability vs. Capacity

Babies learn to walk by falling down, time after time. It's messy. It's failure after failure, but at no point does anyone wonder about their ability to eventually learn to walk. No one ever says, "That baby falls too much. She's never going to walk." In fact, we're certain that they will.

We're certain that children have loads of potential in many areas. My mom always told me that I could be anything I wanted to be when I grew up. She was of the generation that was granted limited options: a nurse or a teacher. She reminded me over and over that I could choose anything, and I believed it.

High school graduates and even college graduates don't seem to limit their options based on what they currently know. I recently attended my niece's college graduation, and the speaker made it clear that college had been just the beginning of what there was to learn.

But at some point, adults begin letting their current abilities dictate future possibilities. At that point, we give the past complete power to define the future.

Ability is what you already know, the skills you currently have. Capacity is untapped potential in you. Your capacity in life after loss will surprise you, but first you must anticipate and navigate limiting beliefs.

Journal Prompt

Where in your life are you measuring yourself only by ability (what you already know), instead of capacity (what could still be possible)?

The Brain's Safety Net

Limiting beliefs prevent us from reaching our capacity. Once again, this is due to the hardwiring of the primitive part of the brain. Its one and only job is to keep us alive, and what's familiar is what seems safe. So by all means, the primitive brain urges us to stay in our zone of familiarity. "Get back in the cave!" shouts your overzealous bodyguard, determined to keep you safely in the damp darkness.

Limiting beliefs are self-imposed road blocks aimed at keeping us inside the zone of familiarity.

Journal Prompt

What is one area where your brain keeps telling you to "stay in the cave"?

Write down what feels familiar but limiting.

Uncovering Limiting Beliefs

Beliefs are simply well-practiced thoughts that are filed away in the subconscious mind. Some are beneficial, like the belief that you should brush your teeth. Notice that you brush your teeth without ever thinking through, word for word, why you do it. That proves that beliefs dictate actions, for better or worse.

Because we don't think through our beliefs word for word, it can take extra effort to dig up limiting beliefs, to even realize that they exist. One way to do it is to ask "Why?" like an average 4-year-old. Ask "Why?" at least four to five times, until you can't answer it anymore. You'll likely find a limiting belief.

Yesterday, my client was telling me that her house was cluttered, needed a deep cleaning, and had much deferred maintenance, all of which weighs heavy on her. I said, "Let's say all of that is true. What does that mean about you?" She replied, "It means I'm incompetent."

(This is, by the way, one of the most competent people I've ever met.)

By asking the question, "If that's true, then what does it mean about you?" I was able to uncover a long-held, well-practiced belief that if the home is cluttered, that means incompetence.

Believing yourself to be incompetent would show up in many areas of life. It would be the self-fulfilling prophecy that all beliefs are. If it were undetected and unchallenged, that belief would limit your capacity.

Journal Prompt

Think of one frustrating situation in your life right now. Ask yourself, "If this is true, what does it mean about me?" What belief shows up?

There is a relatively easy way to coax limiting beliefs out of hiding: Simply dream, and then dream bigger. (See Chapter 19 for more.)

Common Limiting Beliefs

Limiting beliefs sound like:

- "I'm not the kind of person who is athletic/smart/ fit/ interesting."
- "At my age, I can't _____."
- "People my age shouldn't _____."

- "I'm too overweight/wrinkled/unattractive."
- "I'm not smart/pretty/thin/good/creative/talented enough."
- "I have never been the kind of person who _____."
- "I can't change."
- "I'm not capable."
- "I simply don't have the willpower to _____."
- "Bad things always happen to me."
- "I'm not worthy of love/success/happiness."

Journal Prompt

Which of these beliefs have you said (or thought) about yourself? Add any others that come to mind.

Challenging What You "Know" About Yourself

I like to snow ski, and I'm okay at it. I should have taken lessons early on, because my muscle memory maintains some habits that keep me as a just-okay, but not great, skier.

So much so that I was certain that I don't ski black diamonds, the most difficult runs. It just seemed like fact. But when I studied the map of our local ski resort, I realized that some of the runs I often ski happen to be black diamonds. It was a limiting belief, and it wasn't actually true.

Which is almost always the case.

Journal Prompt

What is something you've told yourself "I can't" about?

What evidence do you actually have that that limiting belief isn't true?

Another example would be the common belief, "I've always struggled with my weight," and, similarly, "I'm a person who can't lose weight." The truth is that you've no doubt lost weight in the past, so it isn't factually true that you've "never been able to lose weight." Yet how naturally that belief limits so many people.

If I had a nickel for every time someone told me that in their heart of hearts, they'd like to find a companion or relationship, but "at my age…" "With these wrinkles…" "At this weight…" (insert any other limitation here)"…no one will want me."

Or someone wants to find a companion but is convinced that anyone they might find is looking for more than companionship.

Essentially the brain is saying, "Fail ahead of time. Don't even try."

It's too much work.

It's too hard.

You'll fail anyway.

It's all code for, "Stay in the cave. Don't leave your zone of familiarity. It isn't safe."

And the truth is, this is your brain's hardwiring to suggest this. It's doing its job. Thank you, brain. Your opinion is noted.

Flexing Your Mental Flexibility

You are not your thoughts. You observe your thoughts. You understand that your brain is trying to keep you safe with limiting beliefs. So you can kindly and gently thank your brain for doing its job.

And then you can shift into mental flexibility.

Consider how the opposite of that limiting belief might actually be true.

Make your brain answer the question, "What else might be true?"

Journal Prompt

What is one limiting belief you'd like to release?

What opposite belief could you begin to practice instead?

Building New Beliefs

Sometimes we need to unlearn old beliefs so that we can learn new ones. For example, let's take the belief that a cluttered home means incompetence. The first step is to list all the reasons that that seems true. These are all thoughts that make up the belief that "clutter = incompetence."

Think of it as a ladder. The ladder is called "clutter = incompetence," and all the rungs are individual thoughts that make up the belief.

Now take a look at each rung. Some thoughts aren't actually true. Some were never original thoughts; they were inherited. Some of the thoughts are decades old and outdated. Some were once true, but don't fit anymore. Sometimes knocking out one rung of the ladder will cause the entire ladder to collapse. Other times we must challenge each individual thought, one by one.

As we unlearn one belief, we can be learning a new one. Something you'd like to believe can be its own ladder, with its own thought rungs.

Perhaps you'd like to believe that you're athletic. Rungs on your ladder might include that you played tennis in high school. You like to take a walk in the evenings. You have taken some yoga classes. Maybe that beginning pickleball class looks appealing.

Find every bit of evidence you can, and practice those individual thoughts on purpose, regularly.

Journal Prompt

Choose one new belief you'd like to grow into. Write down at least five "rungs" (pieces of evidence) that support it.

Brazilian author Paulo Coelho is quoted as saying, "You are what you believe yourself to be." What's in your heart of hearts?

Living Into Your Capacity

Expect a normal response from your brain when you try to explore what's possible. It will quickly set up road blocks in the form of limiting beliefs. Thank your brain for attempting to keep you "safe" in the zone of familiarity.

And then go after your goals, your new beliefs, anyway.

Don't let the natural, primal hardwiring of your brain keep you from your heart's desires.

It will feel uncertain, uncomfortable, and maybe awkward. These feelings pale in comparison to losing your spouse.

You will make mistakes. You'll misstep. There will be failures. That's the way of it. Just don't mistake *yourself* as a failure.

Welcome failures for their rich lessons. Be willing, even excited, to fail your way forward. It will only cost you some discomfort, and you know how to feel that (Chapter 4). You have nothing to lose, and so much to gain.

Personally, I want to keep stretching, growing, learning and achieving that which seemed impossible previously. Because the only price of doing so is some discomfort, and yet the benefits are significant and have a ripple effect beyond my comprehension.

I'm here, earthside, and the time will pass anyway.

With my final heartbeat, I want to have stretched and grown and achieved my full capacity in this life. No stone unturned. No capacity left untapped. I want to have loved and been loved deeply. I want to have helped significantly, to have inspired many with my example.

I hope that your unique capacity is fully reached in your one, precious life.

Journal Prompt

What do you most want to stretch into during this season of your life?

What would it look like to move one step closer?

SIXTEEN

Identity: The Freedom to Redefine Yourself

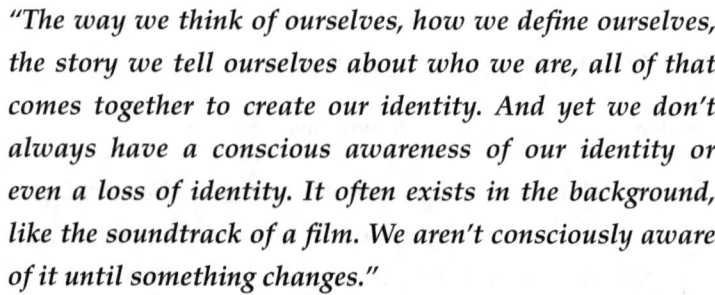

"The way we think of ourselves, how we define ourselves, the story we tell ourselves about who we are, all of that comes together to create our identity. And yet we don't always have a conscious awareness of our identity or even a loss of identity. It often exists in the background, like the soundtrack of a film. We aren't consciously aware of it until something changes."

—Litsa Williams, grief therapist, author

Thoughts Equal Identity

Our identity is made up of our thoughts about ourselves. That's good news, because as we now know, thoughts are optional, and there are an infinite number of thoughts to choose from.

As we grow and change throughout life, our thoughts about ourselves change, too.

Life-altering events happen, like the loss of a spouse, and our identity is called into question. That's how catastrophic it is.

Journal Prompt

What are three thoughts you've always held about yourself?

Which of those still feel true now?

Which feel outdated?

No matter how long ago your loss, your identity can continue to evolve, because your thoughts continue to evolve. There's nothing fixed, nothing inflexible, as long as your thoughts are not fixed or inflexible. Your identity can evolve forever, as long as you're willing to explore other thoughts and try them on for size.

Before and After

The loss of a spouse drops a dividing line into life, delineating all things as "before," or "after." That dividing line can actually be useful when it comes to considering your identity.

I encourage you to consider different aspects of identity, and ask yourself three questions: Who were you? Who are you? Who do you want to be?

Journal Prompt

Write one sentence to describe yourself before your loss.

Write one sentence that describes you today.

How do they compare?

Categories of Identity

Identity can be categorized in any number of ways, but here's a starting point for your consideration, as suggested by grief therapist and author, Litsa Williams:

- **Relational identity:** Wife or husband, mother or father, daughter or son, caregiver, friend.
- **Professional identity:** As defined by your career, job, or volunteer position.
- **Spiritual identity:** How you define your spiritual self.
- **Financial identity:** Breadwinner, bookkeeper, investor, household money manager (perhaps this was an area you outsourced to your spouse).
- **Physical identity:** How you describe your physical self and your physical abilities.

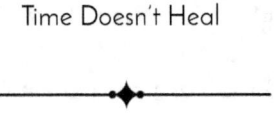

Journal Prompt

In which of these categories has your identity changed the most since your spouse's passing?

In which has it stayed the same?

	I was	I am	I will be
Relational identity			
Professional identity			
Spiritual identity			
Financial identity			
Physical identity			

Choosing What to Keep

Notice the areas where your identity changes from past to present to future, versus where it stays the same. There is no right or wrong answer; you get to decide.

I considered myself Ted's wife, I still do, and I always will. That's how I choose to think about it, because that feels right for me. It may serve you to no longer think of yourself as your person's spouse. Try it on for size, and see how it feels in your body.

Journal Prompt

What aspects of your identity from the past do you want to keep?

Which ones no longer serve you?

The Hidden Grief of Identity Loss

In some cases, your identity changes with loss; this is its own form of grief that often goes unrecognized by the outside world. Tending to this grief is an important part of the journey. Processing these feelings will help you to move forward in a way that honors your past and makes way for a beautiful future.

Journal Prompt

Where do you feel a loss of identity most strongly—in relationships, career, faith, finances, health, or another area?

What feelings come with that?

Who you are now is simply who you are now. Your brain may suggest that this is permanent, or as good as it gets. It's simply not true.

My guess is that this current version of you is learning, growing, picking up the pieces, and doing your very best to navigate the messy middle.

Your Blank Canvas

> *"Maybe the journey isn't so much about becoming anything. Maybe it's about un-becoming everything that isn't really you, so you can be who you were meant to be in the first place."*
>
> —*Paulo Coelho*

Who you want to be is your blank canvas, and that's perhaps a first for you. Not that you haven't chosen your life to date, but that your identity, or some aspect of it, was perhaps by default. You were once a child, a student, later a spouse, perhaps a parent, a professional, etc. We tend to take on the usual identities in life.

The one you didn't sign up for is widowed. I bet you'd trade it in a hot minute, but here you are, staring at a blank canvas for perhaps the first time in your life.

This a chance to reconsider everything you thought was true about yourself.

Journal Prompt

If nothing about your past defined you, what new identities would you choose to paint on your blank canvas?

Stories of Evolving Identity

In her marriage, my client Nancy didn't deal in finances. At least that's what she told herself. She paid the bills, but her husband did the investing and handled the big purchases. She was a person who deferred to her husband for most things financial.

After his death, she felt out of her league visiting their financial planner. But with small steps, she updated her financial identity. She found herself making financial decisions, starting with small ones, and eventually multiple-six-figure ones as she sold their home and bought a new home in an area where she was certain she would thrive.

Had Nancy not evolved her financial identity, she would still be living in an area she found isolating and lonely. But instead, she became a person who makes all the financial decisions, including ones well into the six figures. She let go of her old financial identity, let herself learn as she was able, made small decisions and eventually big ones.

Today she is indeed thriving in her chosen community. Her neighbor is widowed herself, and they've become traveling companions.

Journal Prompt

What's one small step you could take this week to shift your identity in a direction you desire?

Decades ago, Pamela enjoyed playing tennis, but work and life took higher priority. In the years after her husband's passing, she was someone who wasn't physically active. A friend invited her to an introductory Pilates class. Then, another friend invited her to a beginner's pickleball class. She was willing to try, willing to update her thoughts about her physical identity.

Today she's someone who plays pickleball and has a regular Pilates practice. She's now looking for a strength-training class to add to her routine. She's adopted an extremely healthy diet and has reestablished a regular meditation practice. Her physical identity has shifted significantly, with a measurable and dramatic impact on her health.

Expect Limiting Beliefs

Anytime you think about who you want to be in the future, limiting beliefs will instantly pop up. This is the primitive part of your brain putting out road blocks in an effort to keep you safely tucked away inside your zone of familiarity. Expect this to happen, and don't let it stop you from considering who you want to be. When it does happen, thank your primitive brain for attempting to keep you safe, and then shift back into future focused brainstorming. Revisit Chapter 15 for more help with limiting beliefs.

Journal Prompt

Write down one limiting belief you hold about yourself.

Then answer, "What if the opposite is true?"

The Closet of Identity

Identity is simply your thoughts about you. Your thoughts about you are so well-practiced that you don't even think them through, word for word, in your conscious mind. You simply believe them, accept them as factual, and behave accordingly.

Life after loss is a chance to take a fresh look at everything, and nothing is more important than how you think about yourself.

This is the time to take every single thing you think about yourself and hold it up into the light, and examine it with fresh eyes. Is it even true? Is it outdated? Was it ever your own thought, or did you borrow it from someone else? Maybe it was true before your loss, but not now.

It's a lot like going through a closet. You open the door, turn on the light, and then take out one item at a time, examining it for its usefulness, and getting rid of the items that no longer fit.

You may need to unbelieve before you can believe something new.

Journal Prompt

What identity "clothing" no longer fits you?

What identity "clothing" feels right to keep?

The Most Important Work

Learning to unbelieve well-practiced thoughts is time well spent. Ask yourself, "What if the opposite is actually true?" or "In what ways is this not true?"

Unbelieving can happen instantaneously in some cases, and other times it takes practice. In any case, it's worth it.

In fact, it's the most important work of your life. It opens the door for you to achieve your capacity. It paves the way to your differently beautiful life.

Journal Prompt

Looking ahead, who do you want to be five years from now?

Describe that identity in detail.

SEVENTEEN

Path to Purpose

When Purpose Feels Out of Reach

I f you're in the early months of loss and questioning your purpose, you're in good company. It's incredibly common and normal to do so. I often speak to those in the first year of loss and suggest that their purpose, for now, is to be kind and gentle with themselves. To tend to their grief, and to practice unprecedented self-care.

It's clear to me that no one likes that answer.

Instead, we want to be doing something that feels like something. We're human *doings* more than human *beings*. Yet grief asks us to *be*: be still, be quiet, be attentive, be gentle.

Journal Prompt

What might it look like for you to treat yourself as your first purpose right now?

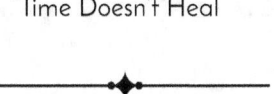

When Self-Care Feels Anything But Purposeful

Self-care feels selfish, after all, which feels anything but purposeful.

But ask any widowed person with a few years under their belt, and they'll tell you that your first purpose is you: your grief, and your needs. It's making your way through the massive learning curve. It's learning to be kind to yourself. Your first purpose is taking care of you.

Journal Prompt

In what ways have you cared for yourself this week?

How might those acts of care actually be purposeful?

Releasing the Pressure to Know

If you're beyond the early months of loss and questioning your purpose, you're likely putting a lot of pressure on yourself. You're likely telling yourself that you should know by now, that you should have figured it out already.

But here's the truth: You're not supposed to know it already. How do I know with such certainty? Because you don't know yet. If you were supposed to know already, you would know already.

And putting pressure on yourself will not help you to know. In fact, it will slow you down.

Journal Prompt

What pressures are you putting on yourself about "figuring it out"?

How could releasing that pressure bring more peace?

Living the Question

Dutch priest Henri Nouwen suggested to "live the questions."

To live a question makes it okay to not have the answers, and instead, suggests living with the questions in a peaceful and patient coexistence.

Similarly, American writer and anthropologist Zora Neale Hurston said, "There are years that ask questions, and years that answer."

Austrian poet Rainer Maria Rilke takes it a step further, saying, "Be patient with all that is unresolved within your heart, and try to love the questions."

Journal Prompt

What unanswered questions are you living with right now?

How might it feel to "love the questions" instead of rushing to solve them?

I wanted to know my purpose, too. It was among my daily prayer requests. I impatiently waited to learn my purpose. I was annoyed with myself for not knowing it yet.

Until one day, my coach said to me, "Teresa, why don't you help widowed people?" It seemed so obvious to her. My thoughts about myself at that time were limiting me, but her words prompted me to reexamine them.

Then it clicked. I looked back at every step I had taken since my loss, and it all made sense. Every step was leading me toward my purpose. Nothing was wasted. I was on the path all along, but at the time, I couldn't see it.

Had my fairy godmother descended into my life to reveal my purpose before that moment, I could not have received it. It would have put tremendous pressure on my already overburdened shoulders. It would have been crushing.

Until then, I wasn't ready to know. It wasn't for me to know. It wasn't time for me to know.

The Power of "Yet"

It's not time for you to know, *yet*.

"Yet" is the shortest, most powerful and underused word in life after loss.

I don't know my purpose, *yet*.

I'm not there, *yet*.

It's not time, *yet*.

I'm not ready, *yet*.

Journal Prompt

Write a sentence about yourself using the word "yet." For example: "I don't know my purpose, yet."

What shifts for you when you add that word?

I'm suggesting that you make peace with not knowing, *yet*. Live in the questions, peacefully and patiently. And even try to love the questions. Trust that when you're ready, you'll know. Trust that in the meantime, nothing is wasted, because you're on the path already; you simply can't see the destination, *yet*.

Purpose in the Moments

And in the meantime, seek purposeful moments. Glimmers that feel meaningful to you. Notice when time passes without your awareness, as painters often say it does when they're painting. These are clues.

Set your intentions at the beginning of your day that you'll find purposeful moments. What we look for we find.

Journal Prompt

Recall one small moment recently that felt purposeful or meaningful. What about it felt that way?

Purpose Evolves

Purpose shifts and evolves over time, and we should allow for that. I believe my purpose is to help widowed people rebuild their lives, and for me, there's no greater honor. And that is one part of my purpose; there are others that feel equally important.

So finding purpose is not a one and done, check the box, mark it as accomplished. It's a matter of what feels purposeful to you these days, and allowing for that to evolve.

Journal Prompt

Looking ahead, what feels purposeful to you today?

How might that evolve over the next year?

The Purpose of Presence

Before his death, Gina's husband spent 40 days hospitalized—ironically in the very place where he had once trained as a medical resident. She vividly remembers a friend dropping by to visit with her in the waiting room. This friend was widowed herself, and her presence so profoundly affected Gina that, to this day, she remembers what her friend was wearing. It wasn't anything she said that was so impactful. It was her presence. It was that she survived her husband's death. "If she can do this," Gina thought, "I can do it, too."

Sometimes your very presence is that powerful. Sometimes our purpose is our very existence on the other side of our darkest days. Without knowing it, we're an example of what's possible.

Allow for the possibility that you have a purpose without fully understanding it or its impact on others.

As my friend Dr. Roger Landry often says, "If you have a pulse, you have a purpose."

Journal Prompt

Who in your life might find hope just by seeing that you're surviving?

How could your presence be purposeful without you even realizing it?

EIGHTEEN

Post-Traumatic Growth

When Growth Feels Wrong

I f the words "Post-Traumatic Growth" (PTG) make you want to barf, I get it.

No one wants to use their person's death for any purpose, and certainly not as a springboard for their own growth.

The day I met Sari in upstate New York, we had an instant connection. Widowed herself, she quickly became a friend and mentor. She said to me, "Teresa, it makes you a better person." To which I replied, "Where do I sign up to be a lesser person?" It turns out, there's no sign-up sheet.

Your spouse died, and that shapes every single thing about your life, including and especially, you.

Journal Prompt

How do you feel when you hear the phrase "post-traumatic growth"?

Does it feel uncomfortable, hopeful, or something else?

Growth is Not Required

That said, growth isn't necessarily the goal, and there's no moral high ground. There's no one "right" way and you're not required to turn your pain into purpose.

But it's also not wrong or disrespectful to grow.

It's not that you would use your person's death to catapult your own growth. It's that your person died, resulting in many awful outcomes— plus some not-awful ones, including that you could grow.

I sincerely hope that my death doesn't mean only awful things for the people I love. I hope that my life on Earth influenced them in good and beneficial ways. And when my life here is over, I can only hope that I can continue to affect them in good and beneficial ways.

Journal Prompt

What would your person hope for you in terms of how you live your life moving forward?

What Research Shows

Research on PTG began in the late 1970s on prisoners of war. Sixty-one percent of the POWs studied indicated that they had experienced beneficial changes as a result of their captivity, while only 30 percent of the control group reported this. (The control group were veterans who spent time in Southeast Asia but had not been captured.)

William H. Sledge, Jams A. Boydstun and Alton J. Rabe, "Self-Concept Changes Related to War Captivity," *Archives of General Psychiatry* 37, no. 4 (1980): 430-33, did:10.1001/arch-psyc.1980.01780170072008.

The findings suggested that suffering was something of a catalyst that prompted people to find new meaning.

Other early PTG researchers studied widowed people.

Continued research showed that experiencing growth in the wake of trauma is common, specifically in the following five areas: increased inner strength, an openness to new possibilities in life, closer and often deeper relationships with friends and family, an enhanced appreciation for life, and a greater sense of spirituality.

Lawrence G. Calhoun and Richard G. Tedeschi, "Positive Aspects of Critical Life Problems: Recollections of Grief," *Omega* 20, no. 4 (1989-90): 265-72.

One does not need to be diagnosed with PTSD to experience post-traumatic growth. But one does have to have experienced trauma.

"Growth is a rethinking, a reassessment of yourself and the world. You don't need to go through that if everything still makes sense to you," said early PTG researcher Richard Tedeschi.

Journal Prompt

Looking back, has your loss caused you to see yourself, life, or the world differently?

If so, in what ways?

Resources for the Journey

Early PTG research was groundbreaking but got little attention, though today one can find far more resources on the topic. My favorite book on PTG is *Upside: The New Science of Post-Traumatic Growth* by Jim Rendon, whose father was a Holocaust survivor.

In short, growth after trauma is common, and it may happen to you.

Holding Both Grief and Growth

If you do find yourself having grown, and you'd trade it all to have your person back, you're in good company. Most people would, including me.

But if the shoe were on the other foot, I would want my death to eventually facilitate growth in the people who love me most. The last thing I would want would be for them to be stuck and suffering out of some misguided allegiance to me.

If my life is complete, by all means, live yours, and live it fully. Grow to reach your full potential. If my death prompts some of that growth, then all the better, because it gives further meaning to my life, too.

Of course, grieve, and be gentle with yourself as you do. And then grow. Become a better version of yourself, and never stop growing. Love, me.

———————◆———————

Journal Prompt

If your person could write you a letter today, what might they say about their hopes for your growth and healing?

———————◆———————

NINETEEN

Your Ideal Story

 "Keep some room in your heart for the unimaginable."

—Mary Oliver

Childhood Dreams vs. Adult Reality

Most children dream about the future: what they might be able to do, who they might grow up to be. Their ideas aren't constrained by their current abilities. They're filled with potential and bold possibilities.

At some point, we stop dreaming. We're no longer expected to dream, much less dream big.

People get to know us by asking, "What do you do?" rather than asking what we dream about.

We begin creating goals based on our current abilities, as if we have no further capacity to tap.

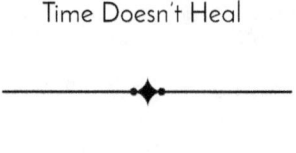

Journal Prompt

What did you dream about as a child?

Which of those dreams still live quietly inside you?

When Grief Halts All Dreaming

Then our person passes, followed by too many secondary losses to count. Any dreaming comes to a screeching halt as getting through the next minute becomes a herculean task. And then the next hour, the next day, the next week, the next month.

The shift out of survival into truly living again is gradual and significant. It opens up the space to dream again.

Journal Prompt

What small signs have you noticed that you're moving from mere survival toward truly living again?

Asking Bigger Questions

What do you want for yourself? Answer that question.

Then, ask yourself, what do you really, really, really want? The answer is probably different.

What's buried deep in your heart of hearts?

Is it something you've always wanted to be or do, something that's been on the back burner for decades?

Or is it altogether different?

Can you give yourself permission to truly live again, and if so, what does that look like for you?

Journal Prompt

Write down what you want for yourself.

Then write what you really, really want.

How are they different?

Permission to Love and Dream Big

Consider that you've not yet met all the people who will love you in this life. Consider that your heart has great capacity to love more, whether platonically or otherwise.

Journal Prompt

If you gave yourself full permission to dream again, what would your bigger dream look like?

Facing Limiting Beliefs

Of course, your limiting beliefs instantly pop up, barriers designed to keep you safe in the cold, dark cave. Expect them to pop up, thank your brain for attempting to keep you in your safety zone of familiarity, remind yourself that you're safe, and go back to dreaming.

Journal Prompt

What limiting belief shows up when you start to dream?

How can you gently challenge it?

Meeting Your Future Self

Imagine a future version of you who has an incredible life. Future You has everything you could possibly want. Future You feels the feelings you'd like to feel more of. Future You does the things you'd like to do. Future You created results that are mind-blowingly good.

Get to know Future You, because there is no better mentor than your future self.

In the future, you've already made it through the darkest darkness. In the future, you're already on the other side of it all, full of wisdom, abundance, and love.

Spend time with Future You. Feel how Future You feels. Listen to how Future You thinks and believes. Borrow thoughts from your future self. Get practical advice from Future You's hindsight. Let Future You advise your immediate next steps. Ask questions of your future self. If you're a praying person, do this prayerfully.

Journal Prompt

What would your future self say to you right now?

Write a short letter from Future You to Present You.

Practical Guidance From the Future

I recently asked my client Carol what her future self would say to her today, as she's in the midst of moving to a new state. She replied, "I think she'd say, 'Keep going, you're safe and being guided. It's all so worth it. This is where you belong.'"

Journal Prompt

What practical step might your future self advise you to take right now?

Your future self offers practical advice, too. When I was dreaming about coaching widowed people, my future self advised me to open a bank account, well before I had earned even one dollar. It was a clear next step, delivered in no uncertain terms. Off to the bank I went.

Currency for Growth

The cost of anything you truly want for yourself is discomfort. You might have to feel uncertain, unsure of yourself, or embarrassed. No big deal, given that you've lost your spouse.

A vast majority of people let their brain's natural desire to dodge difficult feelings get in the way of their dreams. They don't go for the promotion because they don't want to feel embarrassed if they're not selected. They don't ask someone to go to coffee because they don't want to feel rejected. They don't sign up for art class because they don't want to feel inadequate. Line dancing lessons would be fun, but might bring public humiliation.

They never come close to reaching their capacity.

Equipped for More

You, on the other hand, have been through the worst of circumstances. You've felt the most profoundly difficult feelings. You are equipped for anything life might bring your way. I know you'd trade it if you could (so would I). But since we can't, we might as well use it to our advantage.

Journal Prompt

What difficult feeling are you willing to feel to pursue your dream?

We might as well dream big, and then bigger, and truly live this one precious life.

Choose this chapter of your life—don't merely settle for it. You deserve every bit of goodness that's waiting for you.

Journal Prompt

If you were to write the next chapter of your life as a story, what would the title be?

How would you describe the main character—you?

TWENTY

Love: Eternal and Infinite

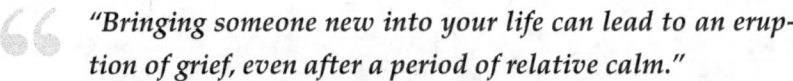 *"Bringing someone new into your life can lead to an eruption of grief, even after a period of relative calm."*

—*Mary-Frances O'Connor, PhD*

Love Lives

When my husband passed, I was certain that his love would be enough for me for my entire lifetime. I felt strongly (and still do) that love is eternal, and therefore his love for me is present tense. I knew that it would more than sustain me.

———————◆———————

Journal Prompt

How do you experience your person's love today?

In what ways does it feel eternal?

———————◆———————

Besides, no one could compare to him. No one could possibly love me like he did (and does), and I couldn't possibly love anyone else in the way I did (and do) him.

I planned to do the rest of my life solo. The thought of being with anyone else seemed wrong, disrespectful, foreign, and cringy.

Love is Infinite

Not long after I had come to these conclusions, my friend and mentor Dr. David Gobble, professor emeritus of Ball State University, was speaking in nearby Yosemite. I attended his presentation and later drove him to the airport. During that drive, he told me that love is both eternal and infinite.

I understood the eternal part, but I had to think more about it being infinite. I wasn't entirely sure what that meant and how it applied to my situation. He planted a seed that day.

Like other messages that are meant for me, it slowly grew roots. Although I didn't understand it at the time, and perhaps tried to dismiss it, it nevertheless stayed with me. My subconscious and sometimes conscious mind examined it, considered it, and tried to apply it.

The heart has infinite capacity for growth. Ted had and has 100% of my heart that was always his. And, somewhat against my will, my heart was slowly gaining new capacity.

In other words, my heart hadn't gotten the memo. It wasn't on board with my brain's plan to live my life solo. As much as I tried to rein it in, it had its own ideas.

Journal Prompt

In what ways have you noticed your heart expanding, even when your brain resists?

Cognitive Dissonance

My heart's expansion launched me into an era of cognitive dissonance, that mental discomfort we experience when holding conflicting beliefs, values, or behaviors.

When we married, I gave my life to Ted. All of my life. When I said my vows, I wasn't thinking, "I'll do this until he passes, then I'll find someone else." We promised to love each other forever and after.

How could I possibly have given my life to Ted, promised him forever and after *and* also feel my heart expanding, adding capacity to love another person? I simply couldn't understand myself.

I couldn't reconcile it. It made no sense. It felt wrong, disrespectful, like I was cheating. I struggled as I couldn't see a way forward.

But the seed that David planted in me was growing. The heart expands in capacity. No one has a second child and therefore loves their first child less. Love is infinite.

Journal Prompt

What conflicting thoughts or feelings have you had about love after loss?

A New Love

I realized that I can love more than one person, at once: my husband in heaven, and earthside, Sonny.

Sonny's great grandmother and mine were the best of friends, and that friendship continued through the generations. He was my neighbor, and the person who grew the hay I fed my horses. More acquaintance than friend before my loss, he became a friend to me as I navigated the aftermath of Ted's passing.

He fixes things for a living, but never tried to fix me. He could accurately see my grief, and chose to keep me company in exactly the place I was.

Confession: As independent and self-sufficient as I've always considered myself, my secret was I wanted someone to ride up on a white horse and save me from the darkness.

The truth, though, is that we save ourselves.

Sonny patiently sat beside me as I figured out how.

Although I was beginning to understand the infinite nature of love, allowing my heart to expand, and figuring out how to reconcile it all, I hid it from almost everyone.

I anticipated judgement from others— which was really my own self-judgement that I hadn't yet identified, questioned, and challenged. They were thoughts in my own brain that I had yet to clean up. Worrying about what others will think is a gift, an invitation to question what we, ourselves, think.

Journal Prompt

What fears or judgments (your own or others') come up when you consider companionship after loss?

In what way do you agree?

Does some small part of you agree?

Support and Understanding

I especially worried about what Ted's kids and siblings would think, and even more so, what my mother-in-law would think. Yet, they were all kind and gracious. My mother-in-law's words were gentle, understanding, and encouraging.

I realize that not everyone has this type of support—which highlights the importance of understanding yourself, your grief, and your needs all the more, so that you can allow others to misunderstand you.

Journal Prompt

In what ways do you need to allow others to misunderstand you?

Living the "And"

It was a decade after my loss that I married Sonny, and I needed every bit of that time. There was a lot to sort out in my brain. That's not to say that my timeline is in any way "right." It was just right for me.

I love Ted and I love Sonny. I ache for what was and I rejoice in what is.

I have Portuguese roots, and the Portuguese are often stereotyped as being a melancholy people. The Portuguese word *saudade* means to have a longing or yearning for something that cannot exist. *Saudade* is always a part of my life, but it coexists with Joy Version 2.0. I carry both. Today I carry them with ease, and I wouldn't want it any other way.

Journal Prompt

What does it look like for you to carry both longing and joy?

It turned out that my original worries were unfounded. Sonny is not Ted; they're entirely different people. His love for me is differently wonderful. My love for him is unique. It's all differently beautiful. If I could put my life before loss and my life after loss on a scale, they would weigh out equally. Yet they're dramatically different.

The day he proposed I said, "I can't leave Ted behind now." He looked at me like I had two heads, and said, "We are going to honor him together." And we do.

There Is No "Right" Way

I share my story not to suggest that there is any moral high ground. Finding a companion or a relationship after loss is not the one "right" way. It's not for everyone, and in fact, it usually means exponentially more work, and therefore more growth.

I encourage you to do what's best for you. That said, I hope you find a way to honor whatever is in your heart of hearts.

I hope you won't let your primitive brain keep you "safely" tucked away in your zone of familiarity by telling you that it's too hard, a needle in a haystack, or too much work. (Ask your brain, "What if it's easy?")

Journal Prompt

What reasons do you want to guide your decisions about love, companionship, or new beginnings?

I hope you won't accept when your brain tells you that you're not young/pretty/thin/wrinkle-free enough, or some other such inadequacy. (Make your brain create a list of what's awesome about you.)

I hope you know and like your reasons for whatever you decide.

I hope you won't let fear stand in your way.

I especially hope you won't let fear of difficult feelings dictate your decision on this or any topic.

Equipped

My brain told me that Sonny will die, too, and I'll fall back into the mire of despair. Why would you even think of signing back up for marriage?

You know how this turns out, my brain warned. It was relentless, as I had expected.

I'm equipped, I reminded myself. If I need to walk through loss again, I have all the tools. I won't be starting from scratch.

I'm equipped. That thought got me to the altar.

That thought prompted me to do the most courageous thing I've ever done—which was to marry Sonny.

Journal Prompt

What's one area of life where you can remind yourself, "I'm equipped?"

Differently Beautiful

As you near the end of this book, you're equipped, too.

What's in your heart of hearts? A new relationship? A companion? A new career? A new hobby?

Go get it.

Life is brutal, but it can also be beautiful. You know the brutal. Don't miss out on the beautiful waiting for you on the other side.

———◆———

Journal Prompt

What's one "beautiful" possibility you want to pursue?

———◆———

TWENTY-ONE

Normal Brain Tendencies

W e humans are the proud owners of these human brains, which are incredible and also somewhat predictable. Whether you're a grieving person or not, your brain will behave in common ways that you can be aware of.

Don't get me wrong: I don't want you to have an adversarial relationship with your brain.

Remember from Chapter 2, the job of the primitive part of your brain is to keep you alive, and every thought it offers you is an attempt to do just that.

If the primitive brain had an on/off switch, we would always leave it turned to "on." There are times that we find ourselves in unsafe situations, such as being in traffic, or walking through a dangerous part of town. Spotting and avoiding impending danger is sometimes necessary. We need the primitive brain to function exactly as it is designed.

Most of us are rarely in actual danger, but the primitive brain is always on guard, appropriately so.

Rather than having an adversarial relationship with your primitive brain, listen to your thoughts, and thank your brain for doing its job.

Then, be "on to" your brain by being alert to the tendencies in this chapter, and following the tips suggested.

Spoiler alert: There will never be a time that you won't need to be listening to your own brain and managing it accordingly. In full transparency, it's a bit of a Whac-a-Mole game. But there is a "leveling up" that happens with routine mind management. (Think "advanced Whac-a-Mole.")

Just as there is no finish line for grief, there is no finish line for mind management. That's the human experience.

Here are common brain patterns for all humans, grieving and not, what to watch out for, and what to do about each.

Self-Criticism

We covered this in Chapter 1, but it bears repeating because it's likely the most common type of thinking you'll experience.

How to Spot It

Become a better and better eavesdropper on your own brain. Use a journal and jot down what you hear. How do you talk to yourself when things are going well? When things are difficult? When you fail? When you accomplish something? When you don't show up as the best version of yourself, and when you do?

How you talk to yourself is habitual, and like any habit, it can be changed.

What to Do About It

When you overhear self-criticism, the first step is not to criticize yourself because you're criticizing yourself. By all means, let's avoid that spiral. Instead, say this, "I hear that self-criticism, and that's well-practiced. But today, I choose kindness, I choose to be gentle, I choose to be loving." Love, after all, is the way forward.

Journal Prompt

What's one critical thought you've noticed about yourself recently?

How could you reframe it with kindness?

Confirmation Bias

I bet you brushed your teeth today. But did you think about why you did it? I'm sure you didn't.

It's because you believe that it's good to brush your teeth. You believe that it prevents cavities and makes your gums healthy. You didn't actually think through the reasons why you should brush your teeth today. You don't really need to, because you already believe it so completely that it's filed away in your subconscious mind. You simply brush your teeth.

And if I told you that a new study came out that says we no longer need to brush our teeth, you would not believe it, because it's not consistent with what you already believe.

This is a good example of how our beliefs dictate our actions. And when it comes to having good teeth and healthy gums, it's great. That belief serves you well.

But I suspect you have other beliefs that don't serve you well.

Maybe that you…

- …aren't pretty enough.
- …aren't thin enough.
- …are too old and it's too late.
- …weren't a good enough spouse.
- …should have been able to save him.
- …no longer belong with a particular group of people.
- …no longer belong, well, anywhere.
- …are failing at grief.

As we've discussed several times, beliefs are simply well-practiced thoughts. (Did you notice how we keep practicing that particular thought?)

The more we practice a thought, the sooner the brain files it away in the subconscious in the spirit of efficiency. Yet, that belief dictates the actions we take.

And the brain will then look for more evidence to support the belief. Plus, it blocks out any evidence to the contrary. That's called "confirmation bias," and we all have it. It's not just a grieving-person thing; it's a human thing, and it's good to be aware of it.

This is why most people don't change political parties. They already believe what they believe. The brain finds more and more evidence to support that belief, and blocks out any evidence to the contrary. Which is why you wouldn't believe that you no longer need to brush your teeth.

Confirmation bias is normal and always in play.

As a person living life after the loss of a spouse, it's good to be "on to" your brain's tendency for confirmation bias so you can find your long-practiced beliefs that are buried in your subconscious mind.

They might be beliefs that you learned as a child and have practiced for decades.

Or, they might be beliefs that came after your loss.

My mission is to help people dig up beliefs and examine them, keeping the ones that are true and serve you well, and deleting the rest.

Let's not let unexamined beliefs dictate the rest of life. Because confirmation bias means that your brain will continue to find more and more evidence that unexamined, untrue, unhelpful beliefs are true.

And that will hold you hostage, keeping you stuck in a mediocre-at-best existence. It's existing, without truly living.

We humans get to think about what we think about. We get to open the door and turn on the light to our own brains, and see what's inside. Take out one thought at a time and examine it—and then choose to keep it or throw it away by unlearning it.

Please don't believe everything you think. The exact opposite might actually be true.

What if you are, indeed, pretty? What if you're not too old, and it isn't too late? What if you were a good (albeit imperfect) spouse? In what ways *do* you belong? In what ways *are* you making forward progress with your grief?

Are you open to considering the exact opposite of your current beliefs? If you are, then confirmation bias loosens its grip on you. You'll start to see other possibilities. You'll set down the heavy burden of suffering. You'll allow yourself to dream again, and then dream bigger. You'll create a life you will love again.

How to Spot It

Notice the actions you take and the actions you don't take. Ask yourself why, and keep asking why over and over.

Journal what you believe about yourself. What are your limitations and shortcomings?

What do you think you're simply not able to accomplish?

What to Do About It

Write it all down, and then ask yourself how the opposite could be true. In Chapter 6, we talked about mental flexibility and the importance of being able to entertain a thought without accepting it. That's not just the value of the Intentional Model. It's also exactly how we challenge confirmation bias.

Our limits are truly only in our minds.

Journal Prompt

What is one long-practiced belief you hold about yourself?

How might the opposite also be true?

Negativity Bias

Are you feeling glass-half-empty these days? If your mindset is doom and gloom, you can't shake free of your spin cycle of negativity, and you can't seem to get out of your own way…I want you to know that you're normal.

To do its one and only job of keeping us alive, the brain must quickly identify danger. Is that a rock in the grass, or a snake? Best to assume it's a snake, to err on the side of caution. Assuming it's a snake is the safer option.

This hardwiring kept our ancestors safe for generations, during times when real danger was truly around every corner.

Although today you're not likely to have a snake encounter, your hard-wired primitive brain is always on the lookout, constantly analyzing situations and quickly categorizing that which is safe or potentially dangerous.

So, it's no surprise that brains are good at finding the negative.

Now add grief, and you've got a brain operating on overdrive, certain that danger is everywhere, constantly seeking and readily finding the negative.

This tendency is called negativity bias, and it is nothing more than our primitive brains doing their best to keep us alive.

Even if you were a naturally positive person before your loss, remember, your brain has been through a lot. It continues to rewire itself to adapt to your new reality, and it will err on the side of caution. Nothing has gone wrong; your primitive brain's just protecting you the best way it knows how.

How to Spot It

Eavesdrop on your own thoughts. If your brain is offering you that you're failing, grieving incorrectly, wallowing, back at square one or other forms of negativity about yourself or others, you are experiencing negativity bias, and that's normal.

What to Do About It

We can recognize the primitive brain's focus on the negative, understand why that's happening, and then intentionally change the channel.

The first step is to acknowledge the efforts of the primitive brain and then demand equal airtime for what's right, what's working, what's positive.

Once we recognize our bias toward negativity and understand why we have it, we realize how much control we have over our mindset.

Allow your brain to tell you all that is negative, difficult and just plain wrong. Write it all down. Acknowledge it with no judgement.

Then, direct your brain to change the channel. What else is true? Where are there glimmers of goodness, even in this life after loss? If you direct your brain to look, it will find them.

Now, you're still entitled to your grief even if you have goodness and blessings in your life. The positive and negative coexist, and they're equally true at the very same time. That's the duality of life after loss.

Just be sure that the negative isn't getting all the airtime.

Journal Prompt

What negatives is your brain focused on right now?

What else is equally true and positive?

Absolute Thinking

With absolute thinking, there's a lot of pressure to make a decision, and there are seemingly only two options. This is because the human brain is skilled at quickly categorizing things into two simple categories (which originally were "safety" and "danger.") Once again, it's our primitive brain hardwiring at work. Once again, the brain is functioning according to its design, and we can be grateful that it's doing its job. Recognition and gratitude are the first steps.

How to Spot It

Notice when your brain offers you only two options: Black or white. Right or wrong. Left or right. Pay off the house or keep the mortgage. Move or don't. Take down the pictures or leave them up. Take off your wedding ring or continue to wear it.

Also be on the lookout for catch-22's—no-win situations that might sound like:

- "I don't want to spend the rest of my life alone, but I can't stand the thought of being with anyone."
- "I know I should go to the party, but it's the last thing I want to do."
- "I want to join a grief group, but I don't want to focus on my grief."

What to Do About It

Ask yourself a few key questions:

- Is this decision reversible?
- Are these really the only two options?
- What other possibilities exist?
- What else am I not considering?

Although the brain offers black and white, the truth is that there are many shades of gray that exist. It's a matter of making your brain see those shades of gray.

Paying off the mortgage is a reversible decision. Downsizing is certainly an option, and so is getting a roommate. You can go to the party for 15 minutes, and then leave, and the same is true for a grief group. You can enjoy companionship without a relationship. You can take your ring off and then put it back on. You can put a picture in a drawer and then get it back out.

The middle ground is probably there. You just need to ask your brain to find it.

Journal Prompt

Where in your life is your brain offering only two choices?

What middle ground might exist?

Scarcity and Fear

If you're certain that there's not enough—time, knowledge, money, opportunities—your brain is in a state of scarcity, and understandably so. You lost your person and their absence changes everything.

Related to scarcity is fear. Many a widowed person fears having a repairman in the home. I found myself fearful of people I had known for decades to be good and kind people. It doesn't need to make sense. Fear is a common part of life after loss.

How to Spot It

The primitive brain keeps us alive by seeking pleasure, avoiding pain, and always being efficient. Anything contrary to those raises a red flag. It's natural that scarcity and fear are common feelings that grieving people experience. You've been through the unthinkable. Your brain is navigating this new, unwanted reality, and it's functioning on overdrive. Scarcity and fear make a lot of sense. Your primitive brain is like a scared toddler, and your job is to comfort it with love and reassurance.

What to Do About It

Notice your thoughts and feelings. If you feel afraid, as yourself why, and the answer will be the thoughts your brain is offering you.

Or, you may be aware of your thoughts more so than your feelings. Journal these thoughts. Doing so will help your nervous system to relax. Let the scared little toddler tell you all the reasons she's afraid. Listen to all of it. Write it down. Search the list for anything factual. If it's not factual, then it's a thought. Note how each thought makes you feel. Remind yourself that your feelings are coming from your thoughts, therefore, you're not in actual danger.

Then, remind yourself of the reasons you are safe, and the specific areas where there is enough. Make your brain find the safety and abundance that exists in your life.

Journal Prompt

What scarcity thought is showing up for you?

How can you remind yourself of what is enough right now?

Longevity

Newly widowed people are certain that "it will always hurt like this" (and that included me). Even someone widowed for just a few weeks can attest that grief is ever-changing, and yet, they are convinced that it will always hurt like this. People experiencing the second year of loss with its unique challenges are also convinced that it will never get better. Difficult feelings seem to be forever. The brain likes to put a "forever" stamp on all that is difficult, challenging or gut-wrenching.

It's just not true.

How to Spot It

As you practice eavesdropping on your thoughts, notice how much permanence you may be assigning to your thoughts, feelings, actions or results. For example, notice when you feel lonely, and listen for your brain to suggest that you'll always feel this way.

Longevity is a form of "piling on." Meaning that there are two uncomfortable layers: the loneliness itself, and the extra layer of suffering on top.

The wound, and the salt.

What to Do About It

The first step is to simply notice this, *sans* judgement. Then, normalize it. This is a normal brain tendency.

Just ask any seventh grader who sits alone at lunch because her best friend found another best friend. She is grieving a different kind of loss and is convinced that it will always hurt like this. You would tell her that it simply isn't true, and you should tell yourself this, too, as gently and lovingly as you would her.

Feelings are neither forever nor fatal. Not the uncomfortable ones, and not the comfortable ones.

Case in point: Remember the family vacation you saved up for, looked forward to, and excitedly packed for? Not an hour into the trip and someone was on someone else's nerves and the bickering began. All feelings are fleeting.

Say this to yourself, "Right now I feel _____ and that's okay. It's neither forever nor fatal."

Journal Prompt

What difficult feeling seems permanent right now?

How might you remind yourself it's temporary?

Arguing with Reality

This topic is the focus of Chapter 11, but it's worth a mention here, as it's a common brain tendency. Arguing with reality always sounds like, "This shouldn't be." And it brings an extra layer of suffering.

How to Spot It

Early in grief, the brain is like a broken record: "He should be here." "This should have never happened to her, to us." "We should be living the retirement we planned and worked hard for." "Why him?" "Why us?"

And eventually the secondary losses hit. When a grandkid graduates. When a baby is born. When a family member gets married.

Quite naturally, the brain offers, "He should be here for this."

There's nothing wrong with arguing with reality. It's completely normal. But it feels extra terrible. It's suffering layered on top of the pain. It's salt in the wound. It's an energy drain.

What to Do About It

If you feel ready to stop arguing with reality, use this sentence, "This is the part when _____ (insert situation or occasion), and he isn't physically present." It's still a tough pill to swallow, but by using this sentence, you've removed that extra layer of suffering. By doing this, you experience pain in its pure form, not mixed with the suffering brought on by resistance. It's like taking the rocks out of your purse. You still carry a purse, and it still isn't light, but it's not heavier than absolutely necessary.

My personal belief is that my husband misses nothing. In fact, I think he experiences it all even more fully than I do. When he first passed, I lit a candle to remind myself that he continued to exist (my belief), albeit in a different form. I choose this thought every time my brain wants to argue with reality, which has happened many times in the nearly 13 years since my loss.

Journal Prompt

Where is your brain currently arguing with reality?

How might you gently shift the thought to reduce suffering?

It's All Normal, and It's Not Going Away

When horses don't want to leave the barn, they're called barn sour.

I get it. I'm barn sour, too. I'm a homebody. If I could, I'd never leave. But errands need to be done occasionally. Almost every single time, my brain argues with my reality. "I should be done by now." "There shouldn't be so many red lights." "There shouldn't be so much traffic at this hour."

I sometimes notice scarcity thinking. "There aren't enough hours in the day." "There's too much to do."

I observe negativity bias on the regular. "My dog didn't eat her dinner. She must be dying."

I catch myself in confirmation bias, too. Especially when social media algorithms offer me more content consistent with what I already think is true.

These brain tendencies are universal. They show up in grief, and in life in general. As long as you have a brain and a pulse, you will have normal brain tendencies.

When they pop up, notice them, normalize them, and then redirect your brain. Don't make it mean that you're failing, or back at square one, or otherwise doing it "wrong." Simply remind yourself that it's a normal brain tendency, and then take the next step.

Journal Prompt

Which of these brain tendencies shows up for you most often?

How could you respond differently next time it arises?

TWENTY-TWO

How to Coach Yourself

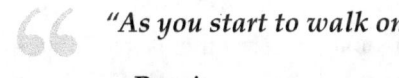 *"As you start to walk on the way, the way appears."*

—Rumi

There's No Finish Line

You're almost finished reading this book, but that doesn't mean you're done grieving. Not when you've finished this book, or the accompanying Journal, or if today is day 366 after losing your spouse. There's no finish line, only the process of getting stronger and learning to carry it well. To that end, I hope you'll revisit chapters of this book as needed.

Journal Prompt

Where do you notice yourself wishing for a "finish line" in grief?

How could you instead think of your healing as an ongoing practice?

As long as you have a pulse, you have a normal human brain that needs supervision and direction. You'll never be finished managing your mind.

But you do have the tools to coach yourself every single day. Self-coaching is an important habit, because you can access it 24 hours a day, 7 days a week. That said, I recommend having a coach to help you when you can't clearly see your own brain.

Why Coaching Matters

Olympic athletes have coaches, because they are so involved in their own brain and body that they can't simultaneously observe themselves objectively and from a distance. Most coaches have coaches for this reason. I can only see in my own brain that which I can see. There's a lot more that I can't see clearly without the help of a coach.

Journal Prompt

What areas of life might be easier to navigate if you had a coach walking beside you?

To get more help in applying what you've learned in this book to your unique circumstances, go to www.thesuddenwidowcoach.com/work-with-me to learn more about coaching for widowed people.

As grief becomes less prevalent in your life, seek out coaching in areas that are of interest, or to help you create a result that you're seeking. There is a coach for just about anything: health, weight loss/gain, finances, real estate, travel, entrepreneurship, menopause, diabetes and all other conditions, and so much more.

Search The Life Coach School Directory (https://www.thelifecoach school.com/directory) and you'll find numerous coaches trained in the very same tools I've shared in this book, who specialize in a wide variety of topics. The tools are universal. My work as a coach is applying these universal tools to grief, but thousands of other coaches apply the very same tools in other areas of life.

The Daily Habit of Self-Coaching

I strongly encourage you to add self-coaching as a daily habit. It's a bit like brushing your teeth: It needs to be done on repeat. I suspect you can find the time to prioritize this important habit if you audit how you currently spend your time. I promise you that if you're willing to trade a few minutes of social media scrolling for self-coaching, you won't regret it.

Journal Prompt

What's one daily time slot you could repurpose for self-coaching?

Here is a three-step self-coaching daily habit I recommend to get you started, but as you gain experience, modify it to make it your own.

Experiment with the time of day you self-coach and then integrate the practice into your daily life as a non-negotiable.

Step 1: Observe Yourself Objectively

What do you notice about yourself today? Maybe life dealt you a new circumstance that set you back. Perhaps you've having thoughts spinning around in your brain. Maybe you can't shake free of that constant feeling. Maybe you keep taking actions that you'd rather not be taking, or you find yourself not taking the actions that you know would be good for you. Perhaps a number of actions have piled up and created a result you aren't fond of. Noticing any one of those things is enough to get started.

Grab your journal and write down your observations. Pick one element: a thought, a feeling, an action or a result, and put it into The Model according to the guidelines in Chapter 3. Complete the other parts of the Model. This is your Unintentional Model.

Journal Prompt

What thought, feeling, action, or result stands out most to you today?

Withhold self-criticism. Look over your Model and withhold any self-criticism. Just notice the cause and effect, which can sound like this: "When this circumstance happened, my brain offered me this default (unintentional) thought, because that's what brains do. And that thought caused this feeling, which naturally drove these actions. And ultimately, those actions created this result."

Be objective so that you don't lock yourself out of the curiosity that is needed. Remember, curiosity will lead to learning. Grieving is learning. Complete as many Models as you'd like, keeping a curious, observational mindset with each.

Journal Prompt

How can you describe your unintentional thought or feeling with curiosity instead of judgment?

Think about what you think about. Do you notice any brain tendencies as described in Chapter 21? Is there a habitual feeling (Chapter 4)? Do you notice yourself attempting to dodge difficult feelings (Chapter 5)?

Journal Prompt

What feeling have you been postponing?

What message might it hold for you?

You're learning to "be onto" your own brain, its habits, its default preferences, go-to thoughts, and, therefore, habitual feelings. The more you eavesdrop on your own brain, the better acquainted you become with it, and the more readily you can redirect it, which is Step 3 below. But first...

Step 2: Process Any Feeling That Is Asking for Your Attention

See Chapter 4 of this book or Episode 4 of the *Life Reconstructed* podcast. This could be a feeling you've been postponing, or otherwise attempting to avoid. It could be a feeling from one of the Models you just created. You get to choose. Is this feeling bringing with it a message for you? If so, write it down.

Step 3: Create an Intentional Model

Keep the circumstance the same as in your Unintentional Model. Then, go "thought shopping." Now, if you've skipped Step 2 above, your thought shopping is going to be limited to thrift stores. Yes, you can find some good stuff, but it takes a lot of time to sort through the junk. This is yet another reason to NOT skip processing feelings. You don't have time or patience for thrift store shopping. Not when you can shop at Neiman Marcus (or insert your favorite store here). If you're willing to process any feeling that is waiting for your attention, you will be able to more readily access high-quality thoughts. You'll have insights that will blow you away. You'll unlock your personalized curriculum that is waiting for you, today. You will level up in surprising ways.

Note that if your nervous system is on overdrive, you won't feel safe enough to process a feeling. In this case, revisit Chapter 2 for tips to calm your nervous system.

Remember, thoughts are optional and infinite. Consider your unintentional thoughts as Debate Team A, then ask yourself what Debate Team B would have to say. Ask yourself, "What if the opposite is actually true? In what ways is this not true?" Brainstorm that perspective.

Shop for thoughts that are true to you, useful, and kind. Try each thought on for size and notice how it makes you feel.

Journal Prompt

What intentional thought feels believable and useful to you today?

Select just one intentional thought from your brainstorm and complete the rest of your Intentional Model (see Chapter 6). Does it create a useful feeling that drives actions you want to take, creating the result you want for yourself? You get to decide.

The beauty here is that the circumstance didn't change. Your thoughts are what changed. You took control of your own power to choose your thoughts. You took control of four-fifths of the Model: thoughts, feelings, actions, and results. That's powerful when, often, we cannot control the circumstance.

But sometimes we can. You can quit the job. You can end the friendship. You can sell the house. You get to choose. But first, keep the circumstance the same, and manage your mind. From that place, decide if you still want to change the circumstance.

Finally, spend time with your Intentional Models. Practice your intentional thoughts. In other words, manage your "air time." If your brain wants to spend time with its unintentional thoughts, okay. And also, spend at least equal time with your intentional ones. Practice your intentional thoughts regularly. Use them offensively, to set the tone for the day, and also defensively, when your brain wants to offer you old, outdated, untrue, unhelpful, unkind thoughts.

As you practice new thoughts, you're creating new neural pathways in your brain. Initially, you'll need to direct your brain to think intentional thoughts, and it will take some effort. At this early stage, the neural pathway is merely a bumpy dirt road. But with practice, it becomes a one-lane paved road, then a two-lane, and eventually a superhighway.

The brain is hardwired for efficiency, so it's happy to travel a well-paved eight-lane superhighway to any destination. Let's make sure it's the destination of your choosing, one that creates the results you truly desire in this one precious life.

———◆———

Journal Prompt

What true intentional thought do you want to practice until it becomes your "superhighway"?

———◆———

Onward

"I trust the next chapter because I know the author."

—Mary Morrissey

Too many people never reach their full potential in this life because of their fear of difficult feelings. They don't apply for the promotion, afraid of rejection. They don't ask someone for coffee, afraid of embarrassment. They don't go for the degree, or finally learn the thing they've always wanted to learn.

"It's too risky," the primitive brain insists. "Better to stay in the cave."

But you've lived the worst-case scenario. You've walked through the darkest darkness. And now, you've equipped yourself with tools to face any circumstance, feel any feeling, and keep stepping forward toward the life that's waiting for you.

Maybe that means starting a business, and feeling uncertainty. Signing up for a class and embracing the nerves of being a beginner. Traveling to a country where you don't speak the language and choosing to feel perplexed at times. Inviting someone for coffee and leaning into the awkwardness.

These are not stop signs. They're tickets. Difficult feelings are the currency of a fully lived life. And compared to the loss you've already endured, embarrassment, frustration, or insecurity are small prices to pay. Every time you process one of them, you make an investment in the life you're building.

The real risk isn't rejection, awkwardness, or failure. The real risk is never fully living again. Settling into a mundane, mediocre, *Groundhog Day* existence.

But you're here. You have a pulse. Which means you have a purpose. You have untapped potential. You have dreams waiting inside you. And now, you have the tools to pursue them—to create an unbelievably beautiful, full, meaningful life.

A life fueled by the love of your spouse, because love never dies.

You deserve that. Go after it.

Love is the way forward.

Acknowledgments

Writing a book is never a solitary endeavor. Though the words on these pages are mine, they are held up by the love, wisdom, and encouragement of many.

Ted, who remains by my side and loves me eternally—reminding me that love endures, transforms, and transcends.

My parents, whose unconditional love grounded me and gave me the strength to keep moving forward in my darkest days.

Sonny, who expanded my heart's capacity to love beyond my wildest expectations, and showed me that joy can arrive in the most surprising ways.

To my clients: thank you for trusting me with your sacred stories and your tender dreams. Walking beside you is my greatest honor. I adore you, believe in you, and celebrate every courageous step you take.

To my mentors: thank you for offering your wisdom, modeling resilience, and challenging me to grow. Dr. Roger Landry, Dr. David Gobble, Erma Trowe, Sari Wightman, your guidance has been both anchor and compass on this journey, and I am grateful for the ways you have shaped my path.

Kristen King www.kristenking.com, editor extraordinaire, who polished these pages with precision and sprinkled side notes of hilarity.

Cindy Readnower of Skinny Leopard Media, www.skinnyleopardmedia.com whose calm competence and ready answers made what once felt daunting both doable and delightful.

To my friends, mentors, and community who cheered me on, whispered "keep going" when I faltered, and reminded me that no dream is built alone.

To each of you who has touched my life in ways big and small: this book carries your fingerprints. I am forever grateful.

Resources

Time Doesn't Heal Course https://www.thesuddenwidowcoach.com/timedoesntheal Apply what you've learned, ask questions, get updated resources, and be a part of the Time Doesn't Heal community.

The Sudden Widow Coach www.thesuddenwidowcoach.com

Life, Reconstructed Podcast https://www.thesuddenwidowcoach.com/podcasts/life-reconstructed-a-widowed-way-forward

Soaring Spirits International www.soaringspirits.org offers a wide variety of programs and resources specifically for those who have lost a spouse/partner.

- Soaring Spirits International's Newly Widowed Program and other virtual resources www.widowedvillage.org

- Soaring Spirits International's Camp Widow is a conference for widowed people www.campwidow.org

Grief Share www.griefshare.org is a Christian-based support group for those grieving the loss of a loved one. **Compassionate Friends** www.compassionatefriends.org offer support for those who have lost a child of any age.